My Liverpool

Famous Liverpudlians talk about their city

William Brown Street, 1947.

My Liverpool

Famous Liverpudlians
talk about their city

Compiled by
Diana Pulson

TEMPUS

First published 2000
Copyright © Diana Pulson, 2000

Tempus Publishing Limited
The Mill, Brimscombe Port,
Stroud, Gloucestershire, GL5 2QG

ISBN 0 7524 2150 6

Typesetting and origination by
Tempus Publishing Limited
Printed in Great Britain by
Midway Clark Printing, Wiltshire

Contents

The instantly recognizable Liver Buildings on Liverpool's waterfront, photographed in 1947.

Introduction

Wherever they hail from, most people have an affinity and feel proud of the place where their roots lie; Livepudlians – Scousers – particularly so. We may on occasions take a cynical view of Liverpool, but let someone from elsewhere 'call us', as we say, then it is a different matter. We get all defensive and patriotic. Though, as many of the comments in this book reveal, we may be well aware of our own faults, we are also prone to be optimistic about our future. It is such resilience that is one of the Liverpudlian's trade marks, and this, coupled with the staggering amount of talent which has emerged – and is still doing so – from the city, which makes it unique.

My thanks for the idea for this book, go to Peter Grant, the Television Editor of the *Liverpool Echo* who suggested it over a pint in a pub. I am indebted to him for pointing me in the direction of a project that turned out to be both fascinating and exhausting!

There was no shortage of material and I received the co–operation of some very busy people in responsible positions, who gave unstintingly of their time to talk to me. I found this overwhelming. Not all of them were born and bred Scousers, some had come to work here, fallen in love with the place, and ended up just as proprietorial about Liverpool as any Dicky Sam. Others had first seen the light of day here and never left – and have no intention of doing so. Some of our most famous names of course, no longer live on Merseyside, but moved on. However, in talking to them, their pride in belonging to Liverpool, was just as obvious, as those who stayed.

Once started, it was fascinating how peoples' reaction to the big events and issues of the years coincided. The Beatles effect was tremendous. Time and again people spoke warmly of their respect for Michael Heseltine and the part he played in Liverpool's regeneration in the aftermath of the Toxteth riots. The Militant years were something people preferred to forget.

As a Liverpudlian myself, I have found it a great pleasure to listen to what people have to say about our city. It has been refreshing to hear their views and experiences – bearing in mind that when it comes to national television and the media, our reputation sometimes seems to be mud! Not so ... read on and find out that there is much more to Liverpool than some think, warts and all.

Diana Pulson
Liverpool
July 2000

Acknowledgements

Apart from all the people who took the time and trouble to talk to me, I would like to thank those who dug deep into their archives and family albums for photographs and illustrations, which they lent me.

My thanks for the loan of pictures also go to freelance photographer Terry Mealey, the *Liverpool Daily Post and Echo*, Liverpool John Moores University, the National Museums and Galleries on Merseyside, the Royal Liverpool Philharmonic Orchestra and Peter Shaw for his charming watercolour of the Liverpool Institute's noticeboard.

Diana Pulson is a former Assistant Editor of the Liverpool Echo *and Woman's Editor of its sister paper, the* Liverpool Daily Post. *She is also the compiler of a book of local reminiscences,* Mersey Voices *(Tempus Publishing), which was based on the BBC Radio Merseyside programmes called* The Century Speaks, *part of the BBC's national radio series to mark the Millennium.*

CHAPTER 1
Peter Sissons

Peter Sissons, journalist and broadcaster.

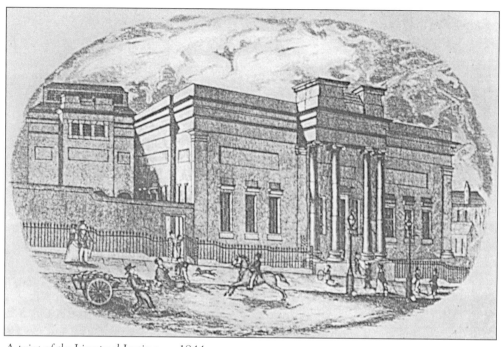

A print of the Liverpool Institute c. 1844.

Until I was eighteen and went up to Oxford to read PPE at University College, I had scarcely been out of Liverpool. I certainly had not visited Manchester, though I had been to the Isle of Man when I was at Dovedale Road Junior School,in Mossley Hill. Each year the top three forms went to Port St Mary for a week. We went over on the boat and I was as sick as a dog, but once I was there I loved it. I was eight the first year I went. We slept in a church hall on palliasses which we had to stuff with straw. In the morning we'd have breakfast outside on trestle tables – great vats of porridge. Jimmy Tarbuck and John Lennon were there, but they were two years older.

For most, Dovedale Road School was a good start in life even though there were fifty three in the class and there was one master who used the stick an awful lot. Today he would be fired.

But we all emerged from Dovedale being able to read, write and add up. Though there was nothing unusual in that. Both my mother and father were at Granby Street School in Toxteth – a tough school in a tough area. Yet they had the most beautiful handwriting and rarely made a spelling mistake or a grammatical error. That was the way people were taught then.

One thing that sticks in my mind about Dovedale is the day I learned I had passed the 11-plus to Liverpool Institute. The whole school was assembled while the headmaster, Mr Evans, read out the names of those who had passed. One by one we went up to take our seats on the platform. If your name was called you knew you had passed while the losers had to go home and tell their Mums and Dads they had failed. With hindsight, I realised how cruel this was and that it might have scarred some for life. But I'm told most primary schools had a similar ritual.

Passing the 11-plus and getting into Liverpool Institute was an absolute turning point in my life. Had I not done so, I would not be doing what I do now, or achieved the things I have.

The Institute, in Mount Street – and where LIPA is housed now – was a terrific school whose legendary reputation lives on. I do not have a single bad memory of it. It was hugely overcrowded because, though it was built for 600 there were 1,000 pupils.

In my time Paul McCartney, George Harrison, Steve Norris and Bill Kenwright were there. So was Derek Hatton, though I was head boy and in my last year when he came into the school. Now, if I meet him at a party, he tells people I used to hit him over the head with a newspaper. One Liverpool politician remarked that I did not hit him hard enough!

Most of the teachers were Oxford and Cambridge men: wonderful idiosyncratic people who were ruled with a rod of iron by the headmaster, J.R. (Jack) Edwards. He had no time for staff of poor quality. They were ruthlessly identified and those who had discipline problems disappeared in a couple of terms. The majority of masters were all scholars who endeavoured to pass on their love of learning to the boys. I recall with particular affection, the late Alan Durband, a teacher of English who had a deep and lasting influence on all those whose life touched his. Alan was later to found the Everyman Theatre. That breed of schoolmaster is now less common, but in my day the Institute was full of these

Pupils at Dovedale Road Primary School, Mossley Hill c. 1959. John Lennon is seventh from left on the back row and Jimmy Tarbuck fourth from left on bottom row.

amazing characters and the results the school achieved were often outstanding.

The year I went up to Oxford, and Fred Brierley was head of maths at the Institute (he later went on to become headmaster at the Holt) twelve boys won Open Scholarships in mathematics to Oxford and Cambridge. No school in the country, including Eton, did that.

It was an honour to become head boy and had great status. When I went to the school as an eleven-year old, the then head boy, Dicky Leach, seemed like a god. He was a great sportsman with golden hair: very good looking, sweeping around in his head boy's gown. Years later, he and his wife invited me to a party. By this time he was balding and middle aged. Not the figure of old but with that indefinable air of the Liverpool Institute Old Boy (Lioban) that we were all stamped with.

Speech Day was a great event, held each year at the Philharmonic Hall. Even today, when I hear the Toreadors Chorus and Gilbert and Sullivan songs the whole school sang, it can bring a tear to my eye. One of the traditions was that the head boy gave the opening oration in Latin. It was written by the senior classics master, D.G. 'Fanny' Bentliff and dealt with modern issues and events in the most skilful Latin prose. In 1960, my final year, I was the last head boy to deliver the Latin speech. Jack Edwards retired as headmaster and Malcolm Smith, who took over, abolished the idea.

'Fanny' Bentcliff, who thought I read Latin out loud rather well (I also did a lot of acting at school) put me in for a Latin Speech

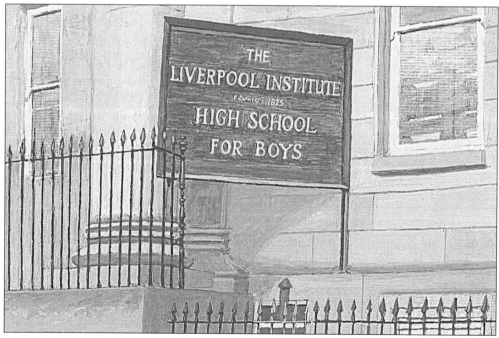

A contemporary painting of the Institute's famous noticeboard, executed by Peter Shaw.

Competition at Liverpool Classical Society, which I won. It may have helped me, later, in delivering the *Nine o'Clock News*, holding my nerve when some particularly arcane pronunciation ambushes me!

My mother was very proud when I went to Oxford just as she was proud that two of my brothers were at Liverpool University and both became doctors. A third excelled in Classics at London University. Father was a Merchant Navy officer whom, because of the war, I did not see until I was three. Mother started work in Lewis's as a beautician, when she was sixteen. It was she who held the family together during the dark days of the war.

School and university vacations meant you had to earn some cash. I had a variety of jobs; guarding turkeys at a turkey farm at Christmas, working in Sayers Bakery. While I was at Oxford I spent the summers of 1963 and 1964 as a conductor on the Liverpool buses. I feel that one of the reasons I have always been able to chair discussions is that I learned the ability to control a busload of Scousers on a Saturday night! There was that frightening moment when you knew you were the last bus out of Lime Street to Speke. There'd be forty people at the bus stop and you'd have to say, 'The first five please.'

When I was born in 1942, we lived in Ingleton Road in Mossley Hill. The lavatory was at the bottom of the back yard. In 1949, when I was seven, we moved to Hunts Cross Avenue in Woolton and for the first time we had a garden.

I met my wife Sylvia, at the Youth Club in St Peter's church in Woolton and when I

Mr J.R. (Jack) Edwards, who was appointed Headmaster of the Institute in 1935.

went to Oxford she went to teacher training college in Gloucester, so we could meet each weekend. Oxford, of course, was a very different world from Liverpool but because it was the Beatles era, Liverpool was a cool place from which to come. You were *persona grata*, especially if you knew the Beatles as I did. Everyone wanted to know you, even if you had not been to public school.

After Oxford when I joined ITN as a graduate trainee and became a television reporter, I would cover stories in Liverpool. I remember going to dockers' meetings when there were 7,000 dockers saying 'Stuff the employers. We want jobs for life.' Today I think there are only 500 dockers yet the volume and value of the trade going through Gladstone Dock is greater than at any time in Liverpool's history. Even in the great days of Empire, no more trade was shifted than it is today.

One holiday job I had was a Securicor night watchman on the docks. It was made perfectly clear to me by a docker's workgang, from the moment I arrived to 'guard' a cargo that was being unloaded, that if I didn't turn a blind eye to the pilfering that went on, something might 'fall' on me.

But being born in Liverpool was one of the best things I ever did. My children (all grown up now) certainly think so because they have the best possible reason for supporting Liverpool Football Club!

From time to time I go back and drive around. My sons and daughter are always egging me on to show them where I grew up … and I still bank at the Woolton Branch of the Midland, 3, Allerton Road, where I have had an account since I was sixteen.

Peter Sissons (b. 1942) has been presenting the BBC News *on television, since 1994.* He and his family live in Kent.

CHAPTER 2
Edwina Curry

Edwina Currie at the microphone for her late night BBC phone-in.

Edwina Currie, a seventeen years old Liverpool schoolgirl.

Babies of my generation tended to be born in hospital and I was no exception. I first saw the light of day at Liverpool's Oxford Street Maternity Hospital. Years later, when I was Minister for Health and I went back on an official visit, someone asked me if I had ever been there before. 'Yes', I said, 'about forty years ago'.

Both my parents were born in Liverpool to immigrant Jewish families who had set out from Russia and the Baltic to go to America, but got stuck in Liverpool, where they made a go of things. My father established a tailoring business in Williamson Square. He specialised in uniforms for ship's captains, beautiful Abercrombie overcoats. He had a love of good clothes and taught me to hang mine up properly – to take them to the dry cleaners. My mother worked with him and they married at the end of the war.

Her family, who were Polish, were very keen on education. My grandparents had ten children and the three eldest were sent out to work so that the others could stay at school. At the age of eleven, I won the Margaret Bryce Smith scholarship to Blackburne House, a prestigious inner city Grammar School. The Margaret Bryce Smith girls were regarded as the intellectual elite who had the future of the city of Liverpool in their hands. Blackburne House meant that though our family were orthodox Jewish, I would not be educated at a Jewish school, such as King David's which was just starting in Childwall. My parents had misgivings about this but I loved Blackburne House, though I did not forget my religious roots. I have an O-level in Classical Hebrew for which I studied at evening classes. I learned to translate the Book of Kings and the Story of Jezebel. I wanted to be able to read the stuff for myself. I did not want it second hand.

Though I liked the fact that everyone got dressed up to go to the synagogue, in Childwall, I did not care for the way the men and women were separated, the men downstairs and the women upstairs. That is where some of my determination to prove myself comes from – the way boys were always favoured.

Unfortunately in the 60s, girls' education in Liverpool – as everywhere else – tried to turn you into a nurse, teacher or secretary. If you were really bright you might be secretary to a bank manager. The idea that you might be the bank manager was never seriously thought about.

Until I was eighteen I had never been far from Liverpool but, in 1964, I was one of the British winners of the European Schools Day Essay Competition. The prize was a holiday in Amsterdam. I met Prince Bernhard, which was fascinating. I had foreign stamps with his head on them. I've still got the scrapbook I kept of that trip, including the sugar cube wrapper!

Politics had begun to interest me while I was at school and I joined the Liverpool Parliamentary Debating Society that met every Thursday at the Municipal Annexe. There were young people from various schools, as well as adults and we debated a motion each week. I was Minister of Education and was addressed as the Right Honourable Member. I remember a wonderful Welshman from the Rhondda who made fiery Lloyd George speeches. It was a foretaste of my parliamentary career to come but though I was interested in politics I did not think I could do it, except as a hobby.

I had permission not to stay for school dinners because they were not Kosher meals. So I'd take my tinned salmon sandwiches to my father's office and eat them with him. Later I'd go to the Cavern, which was going strong, where entrance cost 1s 6d. I'd have a black polo neck sweater stuck down my

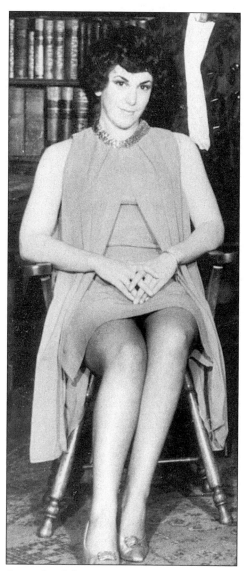

Dressed to kill for an appearance at the Oxford Union, Edwina Currie at twenty two.

Edwina Currie with her mother Pese Cohen, after getting her MA degree at Oxford University in 1972.

sleeve and I would pull it on over my school uniform. I saw all the big groups, Cilla Black, The Big Three, Billy J. Kramer and the Dakotas, Gerry and the Pacemakers. I only saw the Beatles once there, they had already become big business and I saw them at the Empire.

Though I and my friends were at an all-girls school, in our teens, we had the normal interest in the opposite sex. You'd go to a local 'hop' and try to find a boy who did not have too many pimples and was taller than you. One way to get to know the boys at Liverpool Institute, to which we were the sister school, was to choose a subject only taught there, like A-level Maths. Steve Norris was head boy at the Institute when I was deputy-head girl at Blackburne House. We had a bit of a snog, but it certainly was not a romance.

In 1964 some of the girls asked me to organise a 'demo' against a proposal by Liverpool City Council to merge Blackburne House, the Liverpool Institute for Boys and Paddington Comprehensive School into a single site. This was pure dogma because it would wreck two famous schools - the Liverpool Institute that had been established in 1825 and Blackburne House that dated from 1844 and was the first girls' day school in the country. Miss Hooks, the headmistress gave her permission, so I went to the police and told them I wanted to organise a 'demo'. The police sergeant said they would escort us the whole way and would we like mounted police?

There was an enormous turn out. We got a lot of press publicity as we marched down Leece Street to hand in our petition at the Town Hall. The kids from the comprehensive, bless them, held a counter 'demo' carrying placards saying, ' Do Away With Grammar Schools'. Unfortunately, they mis-spelled grammar which rather made our point. But our 'demo' worked. Blackburne House was not closed until 1987 which gave another generation, the chance to be educated there.

When I won an Open Scholarship to St Anne's College, Oxford in late 1964, my parents had mixed feelings, I was moving further away not only from Liverpool but from the traditional Jewish environment they valued. I knew what I wanted. To use a Liverpool metapahor, I felt I had bought a ticket on a ship and was heading out towards the high seas, rather like my immigrant ancesters.

Liverpool as a city was deteriorating fast. Out of my generation 300,000 people left and we knew that if we wanted to make anything of our lives, we were going to have to leave. I had no idea where I was going to end up, but I knew I was never coming back, to stay. I wrote a novel about it *She's Leaving Home*.

Now when I visit my mother in Liverpool I can see signs of hope. Areas like Mossley Hill and the university halls of residence are gorgeous. But half a mile away, Otterspool Promenade is a litter strewn, derelict mess. It looks like part of a Third World country.

Edwina Currie (b.1946) was MP for South Derbyshire 1983-1997. She has written five novels and three other books. She is now presenter of the BBC Radio Five Live programme, Late Night Currie, *on Saturday and Sunday nights. She lives in Surrey.*

CHAPTER 3
Lord Sheppard

David Sheppard and his wife Grace. David, now Lord Sheppard was Bishop of Liverpool from 1975 to 1997.

I cannot think of any city where I would have preferred to be a bishop. It was a wonderful task throughout what turned out to be twenty-two momentous years.

I had visited the city a few times before my appointment. As captain of Sussex, I played cricket at Aigburth in 1953. As Bishop of Woolwich I had come to Liverpool on several Church occasions. When we arrived in 1975, my wife Grace and I, both Southerners, found Liverpool a marvellously creative place. For twelve years, before going to Woolwich, we had been in East London at the Mayflower Family Centre and discovered that London's East End Dock area and the history of Liverpool as a great seaport, had a lot in common.

Among Liverpool's features that captured us were the worship and music of the two Cathedrals, concerts at the Philharmonic where we became regulars and the writers and playwrights, whom we met. There was the lively evening at Willie Russell's home in Woolton; Grace asked him how he came to write about women with such understanding. He said the first reason was sitting under the kitchen table and listening to his aunties talk.

Liverpool is a more religious city than London. It is true that a great many people are 'unchurched – they do not go to Church. But that is quite different from describing them as secularised. I believe there is a widely held sense that there is a God to whom we are answerable. Anglican parishes here have never had the large staffs that London and parts of the South had. But there has been a strong tradition of active lay people.

During the years I was Bishop, I came under extreme pressures. When the Militants were in power in the Town Hall, they said explicitly that they wanted to municipalize all the work the voluntary bodies were doing. After the Militant years, constant squeezes in government spending meant that finding funds to survive became increasingly difficult. Yet the Voluntary Movement has shown remarkable resilience, and, against all the odds, has come through as a necessary and strong arm of Liverpool's caring life. I understood why people voted for the Militants at a time when mass unemployment seemed to have been taken for granted – even regarded as necessary. But confrontation with the duly elected government in Westminster did us no favours. Nor did the Militant leaders' beliefs that they knew what was good for

David Sheppard with Archbishop Derek Worlock.

people and that consultation was a bourgeois waste of time. Co-operation between central and local government, between public and private sectors, and between statutory and voluntary bodies eventually took the place of confrontation and delivered much more for the people of Liverpool.

It was often put to Derek Worlock and me that we became friends and allies because we shared views about social and political matters. We would both have insisted that the central truths of the Christian Faith lay at the heart of our partnership. We regularly prayed together. Producing agreed public statements led on to writing three joint books. The personal friendship deepened. A special memory is of Grace and me going on holiday with Derek and his chaplain, John Furnival. We kept regularly in touch. It sounds stupid but, when we were going to appear together in public, we would check what the other would be wearing – because neither wanted to 'upstage' the other.

Over the years I saw changes in Derek – as he must have seen in me. At first, when he talked about his experiences, I noticed that all the significant names were of Roman Catholics. That changed. As the years went on I saw him caring for the whole community and not just for the Catholic people.

Now that I am retired and Derek has died, both Grace and I miss him. He was a real friend to both of us. The day he was told he had cancer he was due to introduce Grace at the ceremony when she was to receive an

Liverpool Cathedral.

David and Grace Sheppard drink a toast to the Bishop's retirement.

Honorary Fellowship from John Moores University. Despite what he had been told, he rang up to assure me that he would be there – and he was.

The day the Pope came to Liverpool in 1982 was a golden day – with an extraordinary moment when I greeted him in the Anglican Cathedral. The cheering went on and on. I interpreted this as Liverpool's relief that the old bitterness had been put, behind us. We had been threatened that he should not come, with a number of protests and interruptions to services during the previous winter. When the Archbishop of Canterbury, Robert Runcie, preached in Liverpool Parish Church, members of the Orange Order, including a coachload who had come from Glasgow shouted him down.

Liverpool has shown a wonderful sense of unity when it has been most needed. We saw it following the Hillsborough tragedy in 1989 when ninety-six Liverpool fans died. Grace and I were on holiday on the Isle of Barra in the Outer Hebrides. I wanted to know how Liverpool were faring in the semi-final of the FA Cup. When we switched on the car radio, we heard the commentator,confused at what was going on, and eventually telling us the awful disaster. That night I spoke to Derek Worlock in the phone. He told me there was to be a Mass at the Metropolitan Cathedral the following evening. We agreed that I must be there, if it was humanly possible. It was Saturday night and there was no boat or flight that could get me home in time for the 6 o'clock Mass. Thanks to the persistence of Stephen Bellamy, my chaplain, a helicopter came from Stornaway, landed on Barra and took me to Prestwick. From there, a Royal Navy Sea King Helicopter brought me to Princes Dock in Liverpool. My driver, George Walker was waiting and, with a police car that led us through the crowds that were converging on the Metropolitan Cathederal, I made it to the service with one minute to spare.

Some commentators suggested that Liverpool 'went over the top' in those days when the ground at Anfield was covered with flowers. I did not agree. The atmosphere was that of a family preparing for a funeral after a tragedy. Grace got home from Barra three or for days later. She said she felt cut off from the community's grief. She picked some flowers from our garden, went to the ground and placed them on the field. In the services that followed Hillsborough the close partnership of the Church leaders – of the Free Churches as well as the Roman Catholics and the Anglicans – came into its own.

I think of Liverpool as a 'tale of two cities' – Hurt City and Enterprise City. Enterprise City has become vigorous and successful. At the same time large parts of Merseyside have faced deep hurts. In all my years, unemployment filled the foreground. The 'Winter of Discontent ' was expressing bitter feelings. It was only part of ten years from 1975, during which we lost a net 10,000 jobs every year. Now the economy of Merseyside has shown considerable recovery. The New Deal is raising hopes and the government talks of full employment as a possibility.

Particular hurts faced the long-established black community in Liverpool, and still do. The riots of 1981 were, I believe, in the first place a spontaneous explosion of anger against what, with reason, they felt to be unequal treatment by the police. Afterwards, leaders in the black community approached Derek Worlock and me to ask if we would support a request for a Law Centre, This was established, in the next year, offering the possibility that the Law could be a friend to people who had never believed that before.

There is still an absence of black faces in the City Centre, even though I know that some employers have tried hard to open up job opportunities. There is fear about going outside the streets of Liverpool 8 where black people feel safe.

There have been many events that have brought rejoicings rather than hurts. The International Garden Festival of 1984, was something of which every Liverpudlian felt proud. Sadly there were no resources for it to continue. It was a golden year in the middle of some very hard times. There was no litter. Everything seemed to be shining. Grace visited the Garden Festival twenty-six times and, on the last day, one of the workmen insisted on giving her the jacket of the uniform he had worn. She still wears it – quite properly – for her skilled gardening.

David Sheppard (b.1929) was Bishop of Liverpool from 1975 to 1997. He was created a Life Peer in 1998, taking the title Lord Sheppard of Liverpool. During his cricketing career he was capped twenty-two times for England. He and his wife live in Wirral.

CHAPTER 4
Alan Waterworth

Alan Waterworth, Lord Lieutenant of Merseyside. His family roots in Liverpool go back to 1700.

There have been Waterworths in Liverpool since around 1700. Lime Street Station was built on Waterworth Fields, owned by one of my ancestors, Stephen Waterworth. In the directories of his time, he described himself first as a grocer, then as a sugar boiler and eventually, as he accumulated more wealth, he called himself a Gentleman.

In 1871, my grandfather John Waterworth realising that Liverpool was expanding, came from Slaidburn, then in Yorkshire and set up a Milk House, with twelve cows at the back of Mount Vernon Street in Kensington. Housing was developing there so, having milked the cows, he would take his horse and trap round the streets to sell milk. His four sons all went into the fruit and vegetable business which became a very big affair indeed, as Waterworth Bros Ltd. When we sold out to Ross' Group in the mid 1960's we had 250 shops stretching from Caernarvon to Morecambe taking in Manchester and Shropshire. But our head office was always in Liverpool in Durning Road.

When I came down from Cambridge University there was no pressure for me to go into the family business but I still have the letter I wrote to my father asking if he would take me into the company. I started at the bottom – on the shop floor as it were. My first transaction was to sell someone a bunch of parsley for twopence. That was in about 1952. In those days we dealt directly with the farmers from South West Lancashire and Wirral, many of whom brought their produce to the North market which was where the entrance to the Wallasey Tunnel is now. When I began there was nothing like the tremendous variety of greengrocery around that we see now. I hardly recognise some of the fruit and vegetables on sale when I go into a supermarket today! The trade was much more seasonal then and the strawberry season was always an exciting time. I was in charge of most of the buying and we would regularly buy some 25 tons a day at the height of the season.

Dealing with the farmers gave me an interest in farming itself so I eventually bought a farm in Cheshire; though I remained closely involved in Liverpool life. I became a director of Everton Football Club and was Chairman of Liverpool Magistrates for five years and, before that, Chairman of the Juvenile Bench for nine years. It was a great honour when, in 1993, I became Lord Lieutenant of Merseyside. I had previously been High Sheriff but the Lord Lieutenant is the Queen's representative in the county and undertakes the sort of duties for which she would be responsible if she was based on Merseyside. This involves a variety of things, including being patron of over fifty charities and trying to be more than just a name at the top of a piece of notepaper.

One of my principal duties is arranging Royal visits. We do rather well and get about eleven a year. The Queen does not come that often, because she has to visit all parts of the country but she has been twice during my time. The first was when she re-opened the Philharmonic Hall in 1996 after it had been renovated. That day the Duke of Edinburgh had gone off to visit a local factory but had to be back in London the same evening for another engagement. The Queen, anxious not to delay him, got to the airport quite a while before him and seemed amused that it was he who was keeping her waiting and not the other way round.

The late Princess of Wales was here on her last ever official engagement in 1995. At the Womens' Hospital one of the mums put her new baby into the Princess's arms and took a photograph. I have often thought what a wonderful picture that must be, standing on someone's mantlepiece.

Of course the visit made by Diana, which everyone remembers was in the time of Henry Cotton, my predecessor as Lord Lieutenant. It was just after it had been announced that she and Charles were to separate and she broke down in front of the television cameras. In fact it can have been only a fleeting moment because Henry Cotton told me that though he was standing beside her he did not know she had cried until he saw it on the six o'clock news.

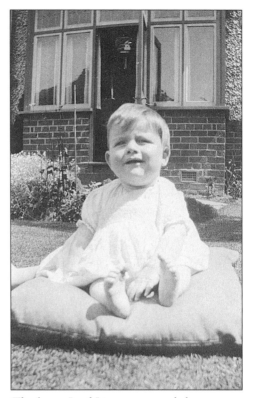

The future Lord Lieutenant as a baby.

On Royal visits I wear the same uniform as other Lords Lieutenant. It is similar to a Major General's uniform, made of dark blue cloth but with silver epaulettes. I carry a curved Mameluke sword – this was favoured by Egyptian nobility in the eighteenth century. Wellington thought they were rather nice and decreed they should be standard issue for British Major Generals.

There are some Royal occasions when I would not wear my uniform. For instance when the Princess Royal was at Aintree for the 1997 Grand National where there was an IRA bomb scare I was in an ordinary suit. The Princess was walking round, talking to the jockeys and trainers whom she knew. Her protection officer got the news of the bomb way before the public announcement and she was whisked away by car. Her behaviour was very cool. The race was postponed until the following Monday when she came back to Aintree.

Before any Royal visit we submit a programme and are visited by a protection officer, not just for security purposes but for more practical advice like 'comfort' stops. If there is a meal involved the menu has to be approved, as all the Royals like to eat sparingly. Indeed the Princess Royal hardly seems to eat anything at all.

Royal visits do not get the coverage they used to which is a pity; and most people are

Alan Waterworth in T.A. uniform.

Everyone knows of the importance to Liverpool of cotton in the nineteenth century. How many, I wonder, know that seventy per cent of the world's cotton is today traded under the rules of the Liverpool Cotton Exchange, which means that all related arbitration is done here in Liverpool. We should be proud of all this – I certainly am. This is because I am a Liverpool man who just happens to live in Cheshire, not a Cheshire man who works in Liverpool.

Alan Waterworth (b.1931) was appointed Lord Lieutenant of Merseyside in 1993. He is a former chairman of the Merseyside Youth Association, Chairman of the Liverpool Bench from 1985-89 and Chairman of the Juvenile Bench 1974-83. He and his wife Myriam live in Cheshire.

unaware of the great interest which members of the Royal family have in Merseyside.

As someone who was born here, I have always loved Liverpool and studied its history. I like its buildings, its people and though sadly, for most of my life the city has been in decline I do get a feeling that things are improving a great deal. Liverpool will have a great future if we make best use of the opportunities that are now available to us. The Port is expanding and the motor industry is expanding here. The pharmaceutical companies are vital to our future, while the part played by our universities in the physical development of Liverpool can be matched by their contribution to the intellectual and commercial life of the city.

CHAPTER 5
Professor Peter Toyne

Frankie Vaughan poses with Peter Toyne after receiving his honorary degree.

Peter Toyne with Cherie Blair, Chancellor of Liverpool John Moores University.

There were 4,000 students when I became Rector of what was then the Liverpool Polytechnic in 1986. Now, at the start of the twenty-first century, and as Liverpool John Moores University, we have 21,000. This is a huge jump and I feel immensely privileged to have spent fourteen years, as the head of an institution which has been able to build up the numbers and offer higher education to so many more people.

Though obviously I had heard of Liverpool, I had never been here until, in 1985, I was asked if I would be interested in the job of Rector. I was Deputy Rector at North East London Polytechnic and there was a lot of negative publicity about Liverpool at that time. It was the time the infamous taxis had been sent round to deliver redundancy notices to council employes – and Neil Kinnock had denounced Militant at the Labour Party Conference. My boss, Jerry Fowler, who had been Minister for Higher Education under Harold Wilson, told me I must be out of my tiny mind to think of taking the job. 'Liverpool is in an awful mess,' he said. 'It's as good as had it. Everyone is writing it off. I cannot advise you to go.' Nevertheless I decided to have a look. I'm a railway buff, so I came up on the Merseyside Pullman, got off the train at Lime Street and someone took me along to the Adelphi Hotel where the interviews were taking place.

The welcome was great. There was a buzz and I decided to take the job, though I knew the downside. Today in the days of tremendous re-generation in the city, it is easy to forget how bad things were. In fact then, the only way for Liverpool to go, was up. Today the Phoenix has risen from the ashes but, my word, there were ashes in 1985 and 1986.

When Angela, my wife, and I were house hunting and wanted to live in Liverpool, an estate agent asked how much we were prepared to pay, Angela said we were thinking of spending £80,000. This lovely guy's reply was 'I could sell you a street for that.' It was almost true. The rest of Britain was booming but in Liverpool things were in decline.

Right from the beginning I was determined to bang the drum, sound the battle cry for the Polytechnic and higher education. Liverpool had been such a wondrous place in the 1960's, now we needed to sell it as a student city and, in short that is what

happened. The minute students started to come, business moved in to match it. New restaurants opened up, the clubs and theatres began to come alive. In 1992, Liverpool Polytechnic – like Polytechnics elsewhere – achieved university status. It gave us confidence. Before that, the word Polytechnic was never really understood by people who percieved it as a second-class place, compared to the more traditional Liverpool University. Now we were in the same market place. Instead of being Rector, I was the Vice Chancellor.

Today overall, Liverpool has 45,000 students in higher education. Fifteen thousand are at Liverpool University, 4,000 at Hope University but the largest number – 21,000 – are at JMU. We employ 3,000 people and have an annual turn over of

The very modern Learning Resource Centre at JMU.

£110 million. I don't exactly know how many JMU buildings there are, but people joke that we are like Rapid Hardware, taking everything over.

When we became a University we had to find the right name. There were suggestions of 'Rodney' after Rodney Street, 'Gladstone' because he was born here. But I thought that as we were a progressive institution, we should not be looking back to the past, but to the future. There was one obvious person who had done a tremendous amount for Liverpool – both in the way of employment and philanthropy; John Moores, of Littlewoods fame. He had died by this time but in 1987 he had been our first Honorary Fellow and been thrilled about it.

In banging the drum we have spared no effort to put the John Moores University on the map and show a bit of flamboyance. Make people take notice of us. Our degree ceremony, for instance, is a big occasion – deliberately so. When I was graduating from Bristol University in 1962, the ceremony seemed boring. You could not say that of the JMU degree ceremony. It takes place in the Anglican Cathedral and though the graduates wear the conventional dark gowns with silver or claret hoods, the Honorary Fellows have gowns of very bright colours that are made in the Fashion Department of the Art School. The idea is that when they process down the aisle they provide a spectacular splash of colour. Its all rather flamboyant – and fun: when Ken Dodd received his honorary degree they made a matching gown for one of the Diddymen whom he brought with him.

Things can get very emotional. Frankie Vaughan was in tears: when he was a child,

his mother, was cross with him for getting dirty and told him no good would come of him. After he had received his degree he raised his arms, looked up and said, 'Momma, what would you think of your little boy now.'

Today three quarters of our students come from outside Merseyside and around 1,000 are from overseas. We regularly go out to Malaysia for a degree ceremony so that parents of students from the Far East, not able to travel to Liverpool, can see their sons and daughters graduate. A group of graduates who studied architecture have even formed their own company in Kuala Lumpur calling it 'L 8' because they had so enjoyed living in Toxteth.

We were delighted when Cherie Booth accepted an Honorary Fellowship at the University in 1997 and when our second Chancellor, John Moores, completed his term in 1999, Cherie agreed to become our third Chancellor.

In my view higher education was a driving force in keeping the flame of hope alive in Liverpool in the darker days. There has never been a prouder moment in my professional life than when the JMU, with Liverpool University, was awarded the freedom of the city in recognition of the economic, educational and social contribution we have brought to Liverpool.

Professor Peter Toyne (b.1939) is Chancellor of Liverpool John Moores University and arrived in Liverpool in 1986 as Rector of the former Liverpool Polytechnic. He lives in Wirral.

CHAPTER 6
Beryl Bainbridge

Beryl Bainbridge with her actress daughter Rudi who starred in An Awfully Big Adventure *at the Liverpool Playhouse.*

Beryl Bainbridge.

Though we later lived out at Formby, I was born in Liverpool and visited it daily. I had aunts in Anfield. Also, my father,who was born in 1889, loved Liverpool and liked showing me round. When I was about eight, we used to play a game called 'Emigration' down at the Pier Head. I'd get on the ferry, the Royal Daffodil and Dad would stand on the Landing Stage, waving his handkerchief, while I sailed across to New Brighton on the Wirral. It took about fifteen minutes. Then I'd sail back.

When I was fourteen, I was expelled from Merchant Taylors School in Crosby. I had been caught passing round a rude rhyme that, incidentally, I had not written myself.

Like Mrs Worthington, my mother had aspirations of me going on the stage and she knew the then Lord Mayor of Liverpool, who knew Maud Carpenter, the manager of the Liverpool Playhouse Theatre in Williamson Square, which had started life as The Star, a music hall, in 1860.

Maud gave me a job as an assistant stage manager. I was fifteen and I stayed for three years; the first two without pay: the final year I earned £4 10s 0d a week. One of my first experiences was to play the part of a young boy in *The Sun and I*. The fifteen years-old boy who was cast to play the role, was refused a license, so I took his place. They sent me to a barber to have all my hair cut off, so that I would look like a boy. I can still feel the clippers they used to shave the back of my neck.

The Playhouse Company was the finest

Repertory Company in the country. The great and the good were directors: Professor Sir Henry Cohen, Selwyn Lloyd, the MP and Lord Simey. At first nights everyone wore evening dress.

There were twelve actors in the company – eight men and four women, including a leading lady and a leading man; a producer, a lighting manager, a wardrobe mistress and Fred, the stage door keeper, who was also the rat catcher. Old buildings, like the Playhouse always had rats, though I never saw any myself. The fact that the actors were contracted for a year helped to foster a team spirit among the company. When I went back years later, there was an admin staff of sixty-five and no permanent company. No wonder the theatre generally is falling apart. Young people coming into the business do not learn their trade as we

did. We did three weeks rep which meant that each production lasted that long. It gave the company time to jell together on that particular play. Maud Carpenter ruled the Playhouse with a rod of iron. When we were out in town we had to wear gloves and carry handbags. We could not be seen in public looking scruffy.

The audience then – I am talking about the early 1950's – was not middle class; but people who had bettered themselves. They were provincial folk who had worked hard and made money. They enjoyed the kudos of dressing up and going to the Playhouse, booking the same seats all the time. There were a lot of old ladies at the matinees.

The Empire Theatre, up the road, was for touring companies, trying out, before going to London. But we were the local rep and we

A sketch of Liverpool Playhouse, by Tim Brakell, 1959.

took a pride in what we did. Don't forget some of the great names of the theatre first trod the boards there, Michael Redgrave, his wife Rachel Kempson, Richard Briers. Before that, when the Playhouse was still the Star Theatre, Lily Langtry played there and Oscar Wilde went to see her performance. In more recent times, people like John Thaw have been members of the company.

As an assistant stage manager, I had a variety of duties. It was my job to go and get the sandwiches from Brown's Cafe. I remember Edwina Currie's father ran a tailoring business from the floor above. If anyone needed a taxi or wanted a bet put on, I had to deal with it. I also painted scenery.

Because I was dependent on my parents I lived at home, in Formby, which was twelve miles away. I'd catch the train from Exchange Station – I went home earlier than the others because I was too young to go drinking. They went off to the Basnett Bar in Basnett Street, just across the road from the Playhouse. They served oysters there.

I have such fond memories of the theatre during those years. There was a wonderful Green Room with a blazing fire and loads of books and props. The kettle always seemed to be on the boil. I suppose I must have been terribly innocent, because I had no idea that so many of the actors were gay. I just thought they were affectionate people.

Later in life, when I had become a full time writer I based one of my books *An Awfully Big Adventure* on my experiences at the Playhouse. It was not only turned into a film but a play that was staged at the theatre.

When I was young, I thought Liverpool, was the most wonderful place in the world. The city centre around Lime Street, always seemed to be lit up. I loved the trams, though you always tried to sit by the door. People did not have baths in those days, so they stank. You'd see children with no shoes and nits in their hair. Those days have gone, thank God, but there have been many changes for the worst in Liverpool.

The Beatles made it fashionable to have a Liverpool accent. But John Lennon did not talk as they do in Brookside. That has become a parody of the way people outside Liverpool think we speak.

My memories of Liverpool which I left in 1963, remain fond, but I don't go there any more. Until two and a half years ago, I tried to visit the city once a month. I'd catch the early morning train from Euston and spend the day walking round, not talking to anyone. One day, I found myself in Hackins Hey which is off Dale Street and which I remember my father describing as the street where all the posh lawyers had their offices. Alas, those wonderful, Dickensian buildings were now in a shocking state of disrepair. The city I had loved for so long, was no more. Someone murdered Liverpool and got away with it.

Beryl Bainbridge (b.1934) has written seventeen novels, as well as works of non-fiction, short stories and television plays. In 1974 she won the Guardian Prize for Fiction with The Bottle Factory Outing. *Her book* Injury Time *won the Whitbread Prize in 1977 as did* Everyman for Himself *in 1996. She has been short-listed for the Booker Prize five times. She lives in London.*

CHAPTER 7
The Earl of Derby

The 19th Earl of Derby who succeeded to the title in 1994.

Knowsley Hall, now a centre for corporate events.

When, in 1994, I inherited my title and the Knowsley Estate from my uncle, who was the eighteenth earl I knew that to use that old expression *Noblesse Oblige*, one had a duty to try and put something back into society and help those less fortunate than oneself, because with great privilege and assets, goes great responsibility.

But my role as Earl of Derby is a somewhat intangible thing to define. Until I got here, I did not quite know what it meant. Basically it is running a business at and around the Knowsley Estate, which includes a park of 2,500 acres and is a substantial employer. There are 170 people employed here, 120 of them at the Safari Park which has the largest turnover of the estate. We have spent £4m on it in the last five years and it attracts half a million visitors a year – more than any other Safari Park in the country. We have the largest herd of African elephants in Europe, monkeys, bisons, lions

and tigers. Our newest attraction is Marcus, the giraffe.

I am also landlord of a large farming community. Many of the tenant farmers' families have been here for over 200 years. They are confined to about six different families. It's a bit of a joke but if you are not born a Hayes, Ashcroft, Cropper or Rimmer you are married to one.

As Earl of Derby, I also have a broader role in the community. Today it is not one of philanthropy, getting out one's cheque book or dispensing beef tea to the poor. It is far more intangible and takes up a large part of my time in the way of meetings and attending events. My uncle was patron, or was connected with, over 200 different organisations. When he died, I felt it was the end of an era and that things could not go on in that way – in John Major's 'classless society'. I decided to concentrate on

Liverpool and the County of Merseyside and have taken just sixty organisations under my wing. They include being a member of the Council of the University of Liverpool, Patron of the Friends of Liverpool Cathedral and President of the Royal Liverpool Philharmonic Orchestra. Very much part of my role is seeing how we can get the whole of the Merseyside promotion together, if we are trying to project ourselves on a national platform and bring business and revenue here. The Safari Park, that was opened in 1971, is something we can be proud of on a national scale. It brings visitors to Liverpool and, as a result, other attractions in the area benefit. At one time there were 25 Safari Parks throughout the country. Now there are just five major ones left: Woburn, Longleat, West Midlands, Blair Drummond (in Scotland) and Knowsley. It takes a lot of hard work to ensure that an estate like this, not only pays its way, but makes a profit. When my uncle inherited in 1948, in times of post war austerity, estate duty was 75%. Now it is 40% which is better. But, if you start handing over 40% of capital value, it digs in fairly hard. I have tried to do what I can to maintain the integrity of the estate, to sell as small a number of pictures and chattels as possible. But I have had to sell some by offering them to the nation. This is a wrench, particularly if it is something which has been hanging in a certain position for as long as one can remember and has centuries of history behind it. But I have not sold a single acre of land, at Knowsley. I am proud of that.

Though my family and I are in London quite a lot because I still do some merchant banking, Knowsley is home. My children, Henrietta (3) and Edward (2) are growing up on the estate. They love the Safari Park, especially the monkeys but we do not take them there too much, or it would cease to be a novelty.

We live in the smaller house that my uncle built in 1966, when he moved out of the old hall where my ancestors had lived since 1385. The Lathoms were there before that. No matter how rich you were, no family could afford to live in a house that size today. The oldest bits you can see are the twin towers put on as part of the Royal lodgings for the first Earl's stepson Henry VII when he visited here in 1495.

Now that the Hall, with the exception of the police dogs, is no longer occupied by the Merseyside Police (they had a lease over about half the Hall and it was home to their covert operations – cheque frauds among other things) we had to decide what to do

The Earl and Countess of Derby with their children Henrietta and Edward.

with it. We did consider opening it to the public but the number of people it was going to take to operate and the anticipated visitor numbers did not make economic sense. We thought of breaking it up into maisonettes or flats – all sorts of ideas from the sublime to the ridiculous. In the end it has been renovated and turned into a centre for conferances, private or corporate parties, filming, weddings and product launches.

My wife, has thrown herself energetically into everything, driving the restoration of the hall through even while pregnant. She used her experience of nine years working for the Queen as Assistant Surveyor at the Royal Collection to re-organise the Derby Collection.

It was not until I was about eighteen, that my uncle started to prepare me for my future at Knowsley. I was encouraged to spend time meeting the tenant farmers, going round the estate and seeing how it worked. But to be

The Earl of Derby's family crest.

honest I did not get to know Liverpool itself until I was about twenty five when I started driving around and visiting the tourist sights. In 1987, the city had really hit rock bottom. The council was unworkable, the services appalling, housing looked dreadful, the streets were filthy, the hotels a disaster. Frankly it was difficult to find anything good to say about it. But since I arrived at Knowsley in 1994, the change has been absolutely dramatic. Derelict areas now have houses on them, tower blocks which have come down have been replaced by better housing. Though the streets are still a big issue as far as cleanliness is concerned.

When I took my seat in the House of Lords in 1996, I made my maiden speech on the Merseyside Economy. As a new boy in the area it gave me the excuse to go round and talk to people like the Lord Mayor, the MDC, the Mersey Partnership and other Liverpool executives from the private and public sector to get a view as to where we were going. The future looks bright. When my wife and I have friends staying at Knowsley, we take them into Liverpool to see the Cathedrals, the Albert Dock, the art galleries and they are impressed.

Of course I understand that as the nineteenth Earl of Derby one might be considered an anachronism in this modern age. Especially as the Knowsley estate is cheek by jowl with deprived areas like Kirkby and Skelmersdale. One recognises the huge contrast, but I am trying to do what I can in my own small way.

Edward Richard Stanley, nineteenth Earl of Derby (b.1962) succeeded to the title in 1994.

CHAPTER 8
Gillian Reynolds

Gillian Reynolds, journalist and critic.

We were a market family. My grandmother had a stall in Birkenhead Market, also one in St John's Market in Liverpool as well as an outside stall in Upper Dawson Street.

She sold 'fents' – the ends of rolls of cloth that you got from the mill. In the war when things were on coupons it was a case of whatever came along. There were big boxes of ostrich feathers, a huge box of buttons.

When I was ten, my mother set up her own business on a stall opposite my grandmother's in St John's Market, selling hats which were not on coupons. She'd found someone in Islington, Sammy Applebaum, who knew how to get his hands on job lots. My mother had a unique sales technique. She took the view that people would look in the mirror and see what they wanted to see. So if she thought they actually looked bloody awful she would tell them so. As a result they trusted her and came back to buy again.

There was nothing quite like the market scene in Liverpool. Traders had passed on their businesses from generation to generation. They were famous for their humour. You started work early and you finished late. My mother, Ada Kelly, knew all the stallholders, but she had a special friend called Ada Stubbs who had a certain mordant wit. Ada sold chickens but so did, Annie Wilson, mother of Anne Robinson, the television personality. Annie Wilson

The rather small Gillian Reynolds with a large array of cousins in 1937.

always wore a starched white overall and a fur felt hat with a feather in it. She looked very crisp and prosperous and was therefore the object of derision to her peers. Ada Stubbs used to call her the Giblet Queen and to this day I still think of Anne Robinson as the Giblet Princess. Because Anne and I were at similar schools, people tried to make us friends but we set our eleven-year old faces against that. Though today we are friends.

The first house I remember was my grandmother's in Norris Green. My mother, father, brother Billy and I all slept in one room. But there was also Uncle Harold, Auntie Doreen, Auntie Pearl, Auntie Nancy and Grandma. God knows where they all slept. It was only a three bedroomed Corporation house. Housing was always a problem. It was wartime and I remember after going with my mother and brother to collect our ration books from the Walker Art Gallery, we went over to the Housing Department. She told us to cry. So we did.

Eventually, and one way or the other, we ended up in our own Corporation house in Parkhurst Road. It was not as grand as my grandmother's, which was a parlour house. We only had a kitchen house – one room downstairs with an old black, iron range and an outside loo. It was in a terrace of eight or nine houses. The family next door who had loads of kids, also had agricultural ambitions. They kept a goat and when there was an air raid they put the goat in the air raid shelter and left the children on the porch.

Because Dad was in the right business, our Anderson shelter had very superior accoutrements. Bunk beds and cork-lined walls to absorb any moisture and ensure it was not damp.

When I was at Monksdown Road School and the nit nurse paid us a visit I was the only one in my class who did not have nits. My mother whisked me out of there and sent me to Broad Square school where I stayed until I was eleven and my life changed forever. I was awarded a Margaret Bryce Smith Scholarship to Blackburne House, the most prestigious girls school in Liverpool. My mother had been determined I would go there for as long as I could remember. She used to walk me past the Co-op Laundry and say 'If you don't do your homework, that is where you will end up. She was a driving force in my life. She helped me learn algebra with sugar lumps. I can remember my tears falling on the sugar lumps as I struggled to learn. We had sugar lumps because my stepfather (my mother had re-married) had gone back to sea and we could afford them.

The Margaret Bryce Smith Scholarship was aimed at spotting Oxbridge potential and putting the successful candidates on the fast track. As a Margaret Bryce Smith scholar you got £8 a term for the first year, then £12, £15 and £18 a term. In the Sixth Form it rose to £20 or £30, which in those days was quite a lot of money. In all I suppose the total was £200 or £300. My mother banked it all apart from the time when I was tennis captain and she took £8 out to buy me a racquet. What was left went with me when I went to Oxford University to read English at St Anne's College.

It always seemed to be cold in Liverpool when I was doing exams. The day I sat the Margaret Bryce Smith paper, the ink froze in

Gillian Reynolds (centre) with members of the Granada Nice Time Team in 1969. On her right is John Birt, then a television producer, who was to become Director General of the BBC.

the ink well. It was 1947, there were four feet long icicles hanging from the buildings. I did not have any shoes, so we took the boots off some skates I had, and I wore those. In the sixth form we had a formidable headmistress at Blackburne House called Betty Bland, who had fierce ambitions for her girls. Originally she advised I should study art at university because she thought my academic record was not good enough. But I was determined to do well in my A-levels and actually moved out from home for a fortnight, to live in a Church of England hostel, so that I could revise in peace. My alcoholic stepfather kept shouting and putting the lights off at home.

My A-level results were good. I got distinctions in English and French though I just scraped through in Latin. The day the

letter arrived to say I had an interview at St Anne's my mother said, 'You'll breeze it, kid; it's on St Patrick's Day.

At Miss Bland's insistance, I went for the interview wearing a tweed suit, low-heeled shoes, lisle stockings and very little make-up. Oxford, was the most beautiful place I had ever seen. I got my place at St Anne's, thanks to the excellent education I had received at Blackburne House. It was a terrific school and now that it is a Womens' Technology Training Centre, it is as much relevant to its time as it was educating the daughters of clerks in 1844, when the school was established.

While I was at Oxford, I came home to Liverpool during the vacation and worked

44

in the market. When my mother died suddenly at the age of fifty-five, I ran her stall for quite a while. It was a good business and among other things, we introduced tights to Liverpool. I particularly loved selling First Communion dresses: they were so pretty.

Life in Liverpool was always changing, but so was I. I was doing reviews of local theatre for *The Guardian* and when commercial radio was launched in 1973, I was Programme Director when Radio City won the franchise.

At the age of forty, I moved to London but found that Liverpool was a place that never leaves you. I used to go on river cruises on the Thames all the time because though it does not smell exactly like the Mersey, it is the smell of a river.

It was the same sort of feeling which in 1960 brought me home from Canada where I was living with my husband Stanley and I was pregnant with my eldest son Ambrose. I realised that if he was born out there he would have no British citizenship. So we came back to Liverpool, lived with my Mum, and Ambrose was born there, as later were my two other sons.

Gillian Reynolds (b. 1935) has been Radio Critic of the Daily Telegraph *since 1975. She is a Fellow of The Radio Academy, The Royal Television Society and an Honorary Fellow of St Anne's College, Oxford. She lives in London.*

Gillian Reynolds with sons Ambrose, Abel and Alexander, 1999.

CHAPTER 9

George Melly

George Melly in academic robes after being made an Honorary Fellow of the Liverpool John Moores University.

The Liverpool playwright, the late Alun Owen, once said that Liverpool was a place that never let you go – and how I agree with that. I absolutely adore it and am always happy to visit the city because it holds so many memories.

Among them are childhood visits to the Palm House in Sefton Park, which fell into severe disrepair, but now, I am happy to say, is being renovated back to its former glory. This large, circular-domed building of steel and glass, was built in imitation of the Crystal Palace. Inside it was warm and steamy, with its own special smell and full of tropical trees and neatly labelled plants. On cold days it was a refuge for blank-faced men in blue suits, often minus an arm or a leg. They were the institutionalised wounded of the 1914 to 1918 war and would sit all day smoking Woodbines on the Victorian benches. The Palm House was my magical palace and its restoration thanks to Lottery money and help from the Rothschild family, makes me very happy.

I spent the first nine years of my life living in a three storey terrace house in Ivanhoe Road, Liverpool 8, not that far from where the Toxteth riots took place in 1981. There were six of us: my mother and father, Tom and Maud Melly, my nanny Bella, a cook and house parlour-maid. There was also my brother Bill and sister Andree. Bella, my nanny had red hair and was given to what my mother called 'moods.' But she was considered to be 'superior', that is to say quiet rather than raucous with not much of a Liverpool accent, though she did say 'buke' and 'luke' instead of 'book' and 'look.' In fact she was so convinced that this was correct, that she tried to persuade me to do the same. Bella was firm, but fair. Every morning she cleaned out my ears with a twist of cotton wool, its tip coated in vaseline, as well as examining my tongue. Every morning at breakfast, in the nursery, Bella and I sat down in front of a different dish. There were fish cakes, grilled tomatoes on fried bread, kedgeree and eggs in various forms. My father liked to eat with me before he left for the office, standing in front of the window with a bowl of Grapenuts and staring abstractedly into Ivanhoe Road. He usually said little but some mornings there would be the sound of intermittent muffled hooting from the tugs on the Mersey, a mile or so away. His response was always the same, 'Its foggy on the river.'

As a family we were posh: up there with the Rathbones and related to the Holts, the shipping family. My grandfather Samuel Heywood Melly, had a chauffeur driven car.

Recently the National Museums and Galleries on Merseyside asked me to participate in the production of a brochure

George Melly, aged ten years.

for Sudley House in Mossley Hill, where my Cousin Emma Holt lived and which is now open to the public. It was great fun and reminded me of my younger days when I used to go there for Sunday lunch. My mother was nervous of this, in case my brother and I were not on our best behaviour.

Emma's father George Holt had amassed a magnificent collection of paintings at Sudley and cousin Emma, who was an old lady by then, used to take me round the pictures and explain them to me. My favourite, was Holman Hunt's 'Finding the Saviour in the Temple.' Cousin Emma used to point out how Holman Hunt had even painted a cataract in an old Jewish gentleman's eye. Then she'd pull out a

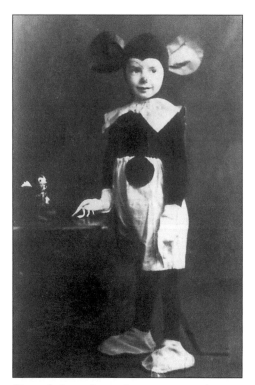

Dressed for a fancy dress party, aged seven years.

magnifying glass and you'd see this huge eye through the glass.

My mother Maud, who later became known as 'Maudie' to her children really wanted me to be Noel Coward. She was enormously interested in the theatre and liked to mix with theatrical folk at Liverpool Playhouse: Bobby Flemyng, Harry Andrews, Michael Redgrave, Marjorie Fielding, Ena Burrill. I met all these people when I was very young because my mother let me stay up and see them when they came to supper on Sunday nights.

When I was four I was sent to a kindergarten called Camelot which was just around the corner from Ivanhoe Road and was run by a short, formidable lady, called Miss Katie Yates.

Though there were only about thirty pupils, we were divided into houses: Percival, Tristram, Lancelot and Galahad, each with its coloured badge sewn on the pockets of our blazers. Life was very pleasant. You crayonned in pictures in a colouring book, moulded plasticine, played in a sand pit, watched tadpoles turn into frogs and did raffia work. One morning, when I was about seven and a half, and in my last term at Camelot, I went into my parents' bedroom and found them looking at a glossy brochure for Liverpool's preparatory day schools. They had decided on a school called Parkfield in Parkfield Road, just a few hundred yards away.

That holiday I went with my mother to George Henry Lee to buy the school uniform, grey flannel shorts and blazer, football shirts and two sweaters, one white, one black, cricket shorts and flannels, black shoes and house slippers, a belt with a snake buckle, a cap and tie in alternate stripes of

George Melly in the Sefton Palm House.

Oxford and Cambridge blue. I was not particularly apprehensive. I'd be home every night and all day on Sundays. It was only round the corner. Now I look back on my days at Parkfield with retrospective terror. The headmaster W.W.Twyne was a big man. Burly but not fat though smouldering with malevolent energy. His rages, which were frequent, distorted his face into a terrifying mask and he would pace rapidly up and down, turning heavily on his heel every four paces. We sat frozen during these performances wondering on whom or how many his retribution would fall.

As a child I would have spent all my time at the cinema, if I could. But there were other activities in which I was expected to take part, like dancing lessons, taught by a Miss Jones, who was so old that she had taught my mother. We learned very formal dances: gavottes, quadrilles, reels and the schottische. We were expected to wear black patent leather shoes with buckles.

We learned to swim at the noisy Cornwallis Street baths that smelled of chlorine and where my mother was always worried we'd 'pick up a verucca.' We were taught tennis by a professional at the Racquet Club, the smartest club in Liverpool, on a wooden court, where under the glass roof, the balls made an incredible noise like guns going off. We went ice skating and, though I did not learn to ride in Sefton Park, I could have done if I wished.

In 1940, after passing Common Entrance, I was sent away to school and that September left Lime Street Station on my way to Stowe. It was the end of that chapter of my Liverpool childhood, but I have kept going back to Liverpool all my life, and always will

George Melly (b.1926), jazz musician, entertainer and writer. He lives in London and Newbury.

CHAPTER 10
Rita Tushingham

Rita Tushingham, actress and film star.

My Dad kept one of those old-fashioned corner shops where they sliced the bacon on a special machine and the cheese was wrapped in cloth. There was also a huge coffee grinder and one of my earliest memories is of the wonderful aroma of all these things mixed together. I can still smell it today. The first shop he had was in Garston Old Road and the second in Macket's Lane in Hunts Cross where we lived.

I never served the customers in either of my Dad's shops but when I was a child I used to go with him on a Sunday and be allowed to stack the shelves. I loved that. On occasions I went out delivering groceries with him. We'd call at all sorts of houses – pre-fabs as well as the posh ones. Sometimes I'd get a biscuit as a reward for my labours.

We used to go to a place called Lightfoots Farm in Hale which was where I fell in love with bulldogs. They kept them and sat them at the table where they fed them jam off a spoon. In all I have owned seven bulldogs. My last two were called Hercules and Brittania, when I was living in Canada. They died but I brought their ashes home with me and keep them in my study. Though I was only seventeen when I left Liverpool it has always been home. My mother and one of my brothers still live in Liverpool.

I went to school locally. First to a prep school called Heatherlea, off Menlove Ave, where I remember being handed in through the window, because I was so small. I must have been about four. At ten or eleven I was sent to La Sagesse Convent where, though I was not a Catholic, I found all the rituals of Catholicism very seductive. I longed to play

a leading part in the nativity play but they were not going to cast a Protestant as the Virgin Mary. I usually played the part of an animal.

I was entranced by all the trappings of Catholicism: the fact that the Catholic girls went to confession on Friday and only ate fish on that day. I loved Our Lady Day in May when the chapel was filled with roses. Then roses smelled like roses and the smell mixed with that of incense was overpowering. I longed to be confirmed at the age of seven as they were, because they looked so lovely in their little white veils.

At the same time I questioned things. I could not understand that when I said that a baby sister who had died at six months was in Heaven, the nuns said this was not true.

The star-to-be, Rita Tushingham with her brothers, Peter and Colin.

She was in limbo because she was not a Catholic. Why, I wondered, because they went to confession, the Catholic girls' sins could be forgiven and mine were not?

With my parents' permission, I left school at fifteen, determined to become an actress. Mum was interested in amateur dramatics so that maybe influenced me.

There was a lady called Mrs Vaughan who did housework for us and I used to make her watch me give a performance, by standing on the window ledge, pulling the red velvet curtains across, then drawing them back as if I were on a stage.

There were two local churches I attended and took part in the amateur drama they did: St Hilda's C. of E. and St Peters Presbyterian chapel, both in Hunts Cross. In one production at St Peter's when I was fourteen, I was playing a character, much older and had to wear a padded bra and be kissed on stage. My parents were asked if they would give their permission!

When I left La Saggese, Mum and Dad sent me to the Sheila Elliott Clarke School in Rodney Street. It was a stage school where you were supposed to learn how to act but also do ordinary lessons. We wore rather silly canary yellow caps – similar to the baseball hats people wear today. My Dad insisted if I wanted to become an actress I must have something to fall back on. This meant a shorthand and typing course at Miss Foulkes, secretarial college in Bold Street, but I was still set on the stage.

After bombarding Willard Stoker, the producer at Liverpool Playhouse with about sixty letters, he took me on as a student assistant stage manager. I thought, I was awfully clever and important being able to go across Williamson Square to Stoniers, the up market glass and china shop, and ask if we could borrow a dinner service for a production. Though life was not always as grand as that. One time I bought a table for five shillings in Rodney Street and another girl and I actually carried it right across town to the theatre. I was there four years but played some small parts on stage as well. Sybil Thorndike, who was appearing at the Royal Court Theatre, up the road, came to a matinee and told me I had talent and should cherish it.

One day I read in the paper that John Osborne and Tony Richardson, the producer were looking for an unknown actress to play the part of Jo in a film to be made of Shelagh Delaney's play A *Taste of Honey*. Bill Kenwright, the theatrical impressario who was then at the Playhouse, and a student ASM and Hilary Crane, the actress, helped me write the letter. When my mother took me to London for the audition she was worried because we saw a cross-eyed woman. She thought it might mean bad luck.

The news that I had been successful came one night when I was working at the Playhouse. Bob, the stage doorkeeper shouted there was a call for me and, when I picked up the phone, it was Tony Richardson who said, 'You've got the part, darling.' I was only seventeen: Dad had to sign a contract giving his permission and in fact I did not start filming A *Taste of Honey* until I was eighteen. Since then I have never lived in Liverpool though Liverpool is what I am and where my roots are.

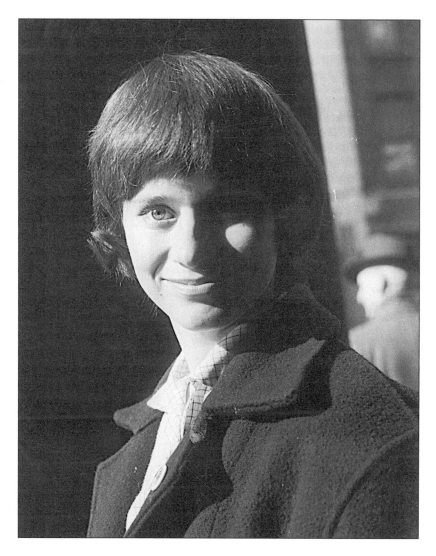

Rita Tushingham, when she appeared in the film that made her name, A Taste of Honey, in 1960.

I go back to visit my Mum and last Christmas when I was home Bill Kenwright, who now owns Everton, gave my daughter and me tickets to watch the Everton match, from the Directors' Box. What a thrill! It brought back childhood memories of going to the match with my Dad. He was an Everton shareholder. I still love football and I am sure that this is to do with the fact of being born in Liverpool, where it is a religion.

Rita Tushingham (b.1942), actress, has appeared in over forty films including A Taste of Honey, Girl with Green Eyes, The Knack *and* Dr Zhivago. *She lives in London.*

CHAPTER 11

David Alton

David (now Lord) Alton. Director of the Foundation for Citizenship at Liverpool John Moores University, against a background of Liverpool's famous Liver Building.

Though it was my privilege to spend eighteen years as a Liverpool MP representing two local constituencies at Westminster I had no idea – or premonition – of this when I first set eyes on the city at the age of eighteen.

It was 1969 and I was on my way from London, where I had been brought up, to start a three-year Teacher Training course in History and Divinity at Christ's College. As the train came over the Runcorn Bridge, I thought we had arrived, but it was not until we descended through the Black Hole of Calcutta, which opens up into Lime Street station, that I realised we had actually got there. Those railway cuttings came to symbolise quite a lot of the things I was to do in Liverpool over the years. The last station before Lime Street is Edge Hill: I had no idea that one day I would be MP for the Edge Hill constituency. I had heard of the Battle of Edge Hill but my knowledge of geography was sufficient to know that that particular Edge Hill was not in Liverpool.

I was already interested in politics and had become chairman of Brentwood Young Liberals when I was seventeen. I knew there were three members of Liverpool City Council who were Liberals - Cyril Carr, Trevor Jones and a man called Reg Atkins. I joined the Young Liberal branch at the Garmoyle Institute in Wavertree and two years later was elected chairman of South Liverpool Young Liberals. In 1970, there was a General Election and Cyril Carr was the Liberal Candidate for Wavertree. I ended up in the college sick bay with blisters on my feet after campaigning for him. I could not walk for several days. Sir John Tilney, the Conservative candidate

was returned. It was a very clean fight. I rather regret that, after this, politics in Liverpool, deteriorated into a much more abrasive and aggressive affair, culminating in the days of Militant. Though I do feel that in the last ten years or so the city has been getting back to where we were.

In 1972, I was twenty-one and still a student, when I was elected to the city council myself for the Low Hill Ward. It was about the time that planners were ripping the heart out of the city and I strongly opposed the demolition of that neighbourhood. It was the last year of the old City Council and there were still a sectarian element on it. After years in power, the Conservatives lost control to Labour but in 1973 the Liberals took over, with an overall majority of forty-three. It was an exhilarating time. By then I was committed to staying in Liverpool and was teaching: but politics played an important part in my life. There were great arguments as to whether peoples' homes in the inner city should be demolished or renovated. I was opposed to the establishment of high rise blocks of flats on the outskirts of Liverpool. I thought people should be allowed to stay where they were. They would have been happy to do that if inside sanitation and bathrooms had been provided. Later, when I became chairman of the Housing Committee, I pensioned off the bulldozer and said we would never again build anything over two storeys high. One of the reasons for this was that I myself had been brought up in a council flat and knew what it was like to live where there was no garden, how easily you could feel isolated and how difficult it was for young mothers to heave prams up and down flights of stairs.

David Alton (right) with Trevor Jones campaigning for election in 1979.

It was 1979 that I became MP for Edge Hill but two and a half days after I was elected, the Callaghan Government resigned having lost a vote of confidence. So I had to contest the seat four weeks later. I did manage to make my maiden speech before the government quit. It was about Liverpool and sectarianism: how I hoped that the Catholic and Protestant churches would attempt to be reconciled and how much our city could teach Northern Ireland. In a way, you could say this was prophetic because, thanks largely to the ecumenism practised by David Sheppard, the Anglican bishop and Archbishop Derek Worlock, and a whole series of Moderators representing the Free Churches, this did happen in Liverpool.

My job as a local MP was to look after Liverpool's interests and there were plenty of local big issues during my tenure at Westminster, which covered the Thatcher and Major years.

Unfortunately Mrs Thatcher was never a neutral figure as far as Liverpool politics were concerned but she made a huge error about the city. It became the enemy for her. It symbolised all that she wanted to destroy: industrial action, wild cat strikes, trade union power, appalling public services, dominated by people who had their own vested interests.

But don't forget that even when they were at the zenith of their power, Militant never achieved a majority of votes among ordinary Liverpool people. If Mrs Thatcher had only cultivated the decent people, she could have become quite a heroine because Liverpool people admire those who will fight their corner. But she ran away from it; she put Liverpool into Purdah and it became like a leper colony. She wrote the place off, which was a wicked thing to do. In my view she miscalculated, but it also served her purpose. If you wanted a museum of horrifying examples, here it was. I had warned in the House of Commons about civic disruption in Liverpool. At the beginning of 1981, Toxteth was a tinder box which could ignite and sadly, within months that proved to be only too true. Apart from general unrest there were *agents provocateur* who were training youngsters to be involved in forms of militancy and extremism, to take on the police and create civic disruption.

John Major who entered the House of Commons at the same time as me, was a decent man who was much more interested in Liverpool. But it was Michael Heseltine, who had a Pauline conversion on the road to Merseyside. When he came up here in the aftermath of the Toxteth Riots in 1981, he went away a changed man. He said in my presence, 'I had not known that conditions such as this existed in this country.' I could see he was moved by what he saw in Toxteth: what he did for Liverpool was a great blessing. He understood the need for massive regeneration. The Albert Dock rose like a Phoenix out of the ashes of the riots. They do say that out of evil some good can come and the Albert Dock development is a wonderful example of that.

David Alton (b. 1951) is an independent cross bench peer and Professor of Citizenship at John Moores University. From 1979-83 he was MP for Edge Hill and represented the Mossley Hill constituency from 1983-97.

CHAPTER 12
Margaret Simey

Margaret Simey, longstanding member of Liverpool City Council and Chairman of the Police Authority from 1981 to 1986.

In talking about myself and Liverpool I think it is important to say that for the first eighteen years of my life I lived abroad. My family were Scots but we went to Cairo where we were British Empire stuff. My father taught in the School of Law and we were very governing class. Because of our education we had to come home and I was sent to St Paul's Girls School in London. St Paul's groomed us all to go to Oxford or Cambridge. We were to be superior women and we were in our day. We were far better educated than most English women. I never got absorbed in the St Paul's upper class ethos. Other girls would say they had to go home at night because they must be in time for dinner which was at eight o'clock, whereas I had to be home for six o'clock, which was high tea with kippers. I learned very early on to keep the two quite separate. They never overlapped. At St Paul's I talked Oxford English like the graduate women who taught us but at home I still reverted to Glaswegian. I am told that when I am angry I lapse into Glaswegian which is very effective.

GRANBY WARD

MUNICIPAL ELECTION, November 1st, 1910.

Miss **ELEANOR RATHBONE,**
THE INDEPENDENT CANDIDATE.

Eleanor Rathbone fights a municipal election in Liverpool in, 1910.

Margaret Simey (second from right) with Eleanor Rathbone (right) in 1929, just after women had achieved the right to vote.

It was only when my father was appointed to be Principal of what was then the College of Commerce, in 1923 that we moved to Liverpool. We lived out at Waterloo, which was beautiful – right on the seafront with lovely, elegant late Victorian houses.

Why I fell instantly in love with Liverpool was that in Liverpool I no longer had to lead a double life. The magic of Liverpool is that it is such a conglomerate of people who all insisted on being themselves. There was a Chinese quarter, the Jewish quarter up Brownlow Hill, the Afro Caribbeans down by the river, the Protestants and the Catholics. I felt like a bird released from a cage. I no longer had to pretend that I was in the governing, educated class.

Fortunately for me, at that moment, the University decided to set up a School of Social Science. I marched in and said, 'I've come. I'm your first student.' They were taken aback but I was very persistent and so

I became the first ever, graduate sociology student. First ever in the world, I believe. The whole course was inspired and, I think, paid for by Eleanor Rathbone. She was the great leader of Liverpool philanthropic life. Her whole family, who were Quakers, had led Liverpool for generations and she had become the leader of the emancipation movement. There were a lot of very energetic women around and they used the Victoria Settlement, down Netherfield Road. It became a club, an education centre, a political a centre. It really was a hub for womens' activities. I got involved in addressing envelopes for Eleanor because she was standing to be a Member of Parliament for the combined universities. It was marvellous fun. Eleanor, bless her, was completely indifferent to class or feelings of being superior. She took everybody as they came. She did not think everyone was equal but they were all of equal worth whether you made a major contribution or took to running a brothel.

As young women, we were full of dreams and ambitions but we were spared the torment of thinking we had to get married, because there were no men to marry. They had all been slaughtered in the First World War. So, while I was a student, we went to all women dances and took it for granted that you danced with another girl. The Charleston and the Black Bottom were all the rage and we used to practice the steps, while we waited for the tram.

In due course the university appointed a young lecturer to teach administration in relation to the people they were supposed to help. His name was Simey and I fell for him because he was a product of Durham and there was no funny business in him about being a superior person. So we were married. In those days, if you were a university wife, that was 'Goodbye.' You went out and lived in the suburbs and behaved nicely, like a lady. They ran a thing called the Ladies Tea Club. I was not at all a success as a university wife.

I struggled on until two things happened: one was the war. Through Eleanor we became key figures in the local refugee movement. In those days you had to sponsor a refugee. They were not allowed in on their own. The University had a terrific record of inventing jobs for academics from Vienna and so on. It taught me about the capacity of Liverpool to take people in. During the war we were in the Caribbean where there had been riots and to which my husband had been posted to 'keep the natives quiet'.

Margaret Simey and her husband, Tom (right) in the early days of their marriage.

When we came back to Liverpool there was this endless suburban life which neither of us could bear. So we moved into the Toxteth area and have been here in Blackburn Terrace ever since. When we came it was a right slum but it has been gentrified and is now really rather grand and economically quite valuable.

At this point I was ready to 'Go' and remember saying to my husband 'It may spoil your career but I am going into politics.' Bessie Braddock was MP for Liverpool Exchange and I became one of her secretaries. By the time I was councillor for Granby ward, I was well trained. I did a lot of voluntary work, became a magistrate and ended up as Chairman of the Police Committee to everyone's surprise. I was already in my seventies. I got very caught up in Toxteth affairs which was why, when the riots of 1981 broke out, I spoke up in defence of the people of the area.

That was where the clash with Ken Oxford, the Chief Constable came in. I like to think that the clash was about principles; it was not personal. I quite liked Oxford. The trouble was that he said the top dog had to be the professional and he would say how Liverpool would be policed. I said 'Oh no! We pay for it, we must have the service we want.'

The night the riots took place, I was in my house in Blackburn Terrace and we could see the flames shooting into the sky. A young youth leader came round in the middle of the night and asked what I was going to do. Next day, I tried to go out but a police officer and a CID man grabbed me – almost arrested me – pushed me into his car and told me to stay indoors. I reminded him

that I was the Chairman of the Police Authority but he told me to leave it to them. That was twenty years ago and Liverpool has been through a few ups and downs since then but Liverpool is still here. The city has a great survival instinct.

Margaret Simey (b.1906) was Chairman of the Liverpool Police Authority from 1981 to 1986 and a member of Liverpool City Council from 1963 to 1973.

CHAPTER 13
Adrian Henri

Adrian Henri, 'Liverpool Poet' and painter.

For me, the 1960s in Liverpool were the most enjoyable time of my life. It seemed as if we were at the centre of the world. Everything was happening here.

The Beatles were starting to make their name but there were other things as well. Three of us, Roger McGough, Brian Patten and myself became known as the Liverpool 8 Poets. Brian and Roger were already doing poetry readings when I met them in 1961. These were held once a week in the cellar at a restaurant called Sampson and Barlow, in London Road. Roger and Brian knew that I also dabbled in poetry and asked me to bring some of my poems along. Eventually I was persuaded to do so and it was one of the defining moments of my life. I discovered that though all the poncey, intellectual stuff I had written sounded fine to me, when I read it out loud before an audience, it was embarrassing. We had all been influenced by T.S. Eliot and W.H. Auden. What I did was to produce poetry which was an amalgam.

The Liverpool Poets were not about this. We set out to be different. We did not use long words. I suppose you could say we wrote in the vernacular. Still do. We tried to produce new poems every week. Sometimes I would write a line, then Brian, the following one. It was hard going but fun.

Looking back on those early days none of us thought that one day our poems would be analysed by scholars, studied in schools and read at memorial services.

I was thirty when I finally came to live in Liverpool in 1957. I got a job painting scenery at the Playhouse Theatre; then I taught art at a local school. I'd taken a degree in Fine Arts at Newcastle University. Later I taught at Liverpool College of Art for two and a half years. It was then I got to know John Lennon. I was a friend of Stuart Sutcliffe, the fifth Beatle and Lennon and that gang drank at the Cracke and at P. Kavanagh's.

John Lennon was a difficult person – very shy. He tended to latch onto people who were his intellectual superiors. He needed the sustenance of those who were cleverer than him, hence his dependence on Stuart Sutcliffe, Paul McCartney and finally Yoko Ono.

No-one who was around at the time will forget the Cavern days. It was a very smelly,

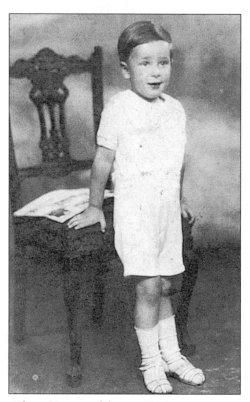

Adrian Henri aged four in 1936.

very noisy place. For a shilling you could get a bowl of soup and listen to a band.

At one point I gave up teaching and formed a rock and roll band myself. It was a different audience from the people who came to listen to our poetry readings. In Liverpool, in those days you simply got on

Adrian Henri performing at the Institute of Contemporary Arts in 1967.

with it. Today people start wondering if they can get a grant and asking themselves if they can make a living with it. We just did it

There was so much going on intellectually in the city. The Scaffold were formed with Roger McGough, John Gorman and Paul McCartney's brother Mike, who called himself Mike McGear. They wrote strange songs like *Lily the Pink* and *Thank You Very Much*. The art world was flourishing. My sort of art, Pop Art – began to be appreciated. Then there was Kirklands, in Hardman Street, originally an elegant nineteenth century bakery, which became a wine bar in the 1960s: possibly Britain's first wine bar, with a music room above. It became a trendy meeting place for everyone – especially on Sunday nights. Being a wine bar it was a bit of a novelty. Before that folk either went out for a serious drink or a cup of tea at the Kardomah.

In those days, the Bohemian crowd of which I suppose we were part, tended to live on the top floors of the big Victorian houses around Canning Street and Falkner Square. Largely because they were cheap and also because they had big rooms. My own house in Mount Street where I live now, was built in 1812. It's opposite what was the old Liverpool Institute where McCartney went to school and where LIPA is now housed.

Since those years the city has been through some hard times but I still feel Liverpool people are unique, particularly in their humour. At one point it was dockers' humour but the dockers have gone, yet there is still plenty of humour around.

The artist at work. Adrian Henri at his easel.

They say that the city is on the up and up and certainly there are plenty of developments and building conversions to support this. But, given the choice, how I would love to go back to the years between 1967 and 1970. It was a period of such intellectual adventure. Lots of people were doing interesting things. More than anything else it was a time of optimism, the feeling that you could do anything. For instance I was past my 30s when I went into rock music, but I still did it.

Mind you I've never made any money. I've lived on a shoestring. But I'm like Mr McCawber: I'm sure something will turn up.

Adrian Henri (b.1932), artist and poet and member of the Liverpool Poets. In 1972 he was a prizewinner in the John Moores Art Exhibition. He lives in Liverpool.

CHAPTER 14

Billy Butler

Billy Butler in charateristic pose – at the microphone at Radio Merseyside.

Looking back, there was a sort of innocence about growing up in Liverpool, as far as my generation was concerned. You were warned about talking to strangers, just the same as kids always have been. But you would think nothing of asking an adult whom you had never seen before, to take you into the cinema, if it was an evening performance. You had to be sixteen to get in on your own.

My Mam accepted this, though she did warn us to be careful who we went in with. Like most parents of those days she was strict but we had an inbuilt respect for authority. For instance, if we climbed over the fence at Newsham Park to go fishing and were spotted by the 'Parkie' (the park-keeper) and he roared at us, we fled. I don't know if kids would react like that today. To get the money to go the pictures, we would do all sorts of things, run messages for the neighbours, scrounge empty lemonade bottles for which we got a penny back, take newspapers to the chippie.

Billy Butler, aged seven years.

My Mam brought me and my brothers up on her own. She did all sorts of jobs, worked in a bottle factory and as a barmaid, ran a kiosk at the Pier Head. But though there was never a lot of cash about, we did not seem to go short of anything that mattered. It was not until I was grown up that I realised we had been poor, in the sense people were in those days. These days being poor means only having one telly.

To say my Mam was houseproud was to put it mildly. She kept the house immaculate and the front step was cleaned with pumice stone and whitened. Then she would cover it with a tea towel. You had to step on that and a nearby grid, to avoid dirtying it. She claimed she was not a good cook, but she made marvellous Scouse and neck end of lamb soups. Though she was terrible at scones. They were so hard they were like bullets. On Sunday we had rabbit and at Christmas there was chicken – but only at Christmas. If we were buying sweets we'd choose things like Tiger Nuts, Sticky Lice and Barley Sugar.

The family unit was important in those days. There were a lot of aunties and uncles. Uncle Paddy and Auntie Dot lived in Dovecot, which was a nice area, so they were posh. Auntie Ruth always smelled expensive.

As I was born in 1942, I was too young to remember the war, but I do recall playing on old bomb sites. As schoolboys there were seasons for certain games: 'ollies' (marbles), whip and top, one where you flattened out a matchbox, put it against the wall and tried to knock it down. If you could not afford marbles you took the stones out of cherries, sucked them clean and used them instead.

Later on you started thinking of girls but we were all very moral. If you knew someone had taken a girl out you'd ask your mate if he had got the top. This meant her boobs. If he said 'Yes' you'd ask 'outside or inside?' That was as far as it got. Myself I was a terrified of kissing a girl the right way. I used to practice by kissing my hand.

When you left school you took what work you could. While I was working for American Express as a Shipping and Forwarding clerk, I started a group, The Merseybeats. We made our debut at Bootle Town Hall and the headline in the *Bootle Times* was 'Big Cigar Man Hits Town.' I'd bought a large fake cigar from the Wizard's Den, the joke shop. You unscrewed the top, and fitted a cigarette into it. It looked as if you were smoking this massive cigar.

I got my chance to break into local radio when a Radio Merseyside producer asked me to stand in for Kenny Everitt for four weeks on a Saturday morning. The basic opinion at Radio Mersyside was that I lowered the tone of the station: that I was too common

Billy Butler and his wife Lesley on their wedding day.

and bit brash. But I started getting mail and, from then on, my career in local radio took off.

The relationship which Liverpool people have with their local radio stations is unique. There is nothing like it elsewhere in the country. The Hillsborough tragedy is a case in point. Radio Mersyside told any listener who wanted to ring in to do so. Wally Scott, and I who were by this well established as a radio duo received many wonderful complimentary letters about the way we tried to help the city come to terms with its grief. We tried to keep the mood low and calm for three or four weeks until we could feel that it was starting to recover. I played music that would be a comfort: songs like *One Day at a Time, If Only I Had Known*. The whole thing was emotionally draining. Wally and I went to several funerals.

As a city, Liverpool is a terrific place but I don't go over board too much about it. There's bad, as well as good here but the people are quicker than most to come forward and offer help. Usually those who can least afford it. Mind you, they don't mince their words. A lady stopped me in the street and said she lived alone and, for the three hours a day we were on the radio, she thought of Wally and I as her family. Then she added, 'I don't understand why so many people hate you.' Only a Scouser would say that sort of thing. Another woman in a fruit shop who recognised me, refused to sell me some apples, because she said I made a show of Liverpool because of the way I talked.

The Scouse accent is a matter of debate. It certainly is not the way people outside Liverpool talk when they are imitating it.

But that does not bother me. One thing that does is the envy that can be found here. If anyone makes it and moves away they are classed as traitors. People have to go where their work takes them. It's not a question of deserting their roots.

Billy Butler (b.1942) is a presenter for BBC Radio Merseyside.

CHAPTER 15

Paula Ridley

Paula Ridley with Harold Wilson when he opened the Students' Union at Liverpool University, 1965.

Until I came to Liverpool to be interviewed for a place at Liverpool University, I had never visited the city so, when I arrived, at the age of eighteen, I did not know much about it.

It was 1962 when I became an undergraduate. I read Politics, and also met and married my husband who taught Politics at the university, so I have been here quite a while – though I'm not sure how long it takes to become a Liverpudlian!.

From early on, the civic life of Liverpool, the number of listed buildings and its architectural history, fascinated me. In the 1970s I became Secretary of the Merseyside Civic Society. This was at a time when people were just becoming conscious of our amazing architectural heritage, though the city and government view of old buildings was knock them down and replace them with anything. We said a definite 'No!' to this. A town without old buildings is like a man without a memory. Not only are they important as an external signal but to the people who live here.

After the battle of the Lyceum in the 70s when we reversed listed building consent for demolition, there was the planning application to fill the Albert Dock with concrete and create a car park, followed by a public inquiry. I felt that if we allowed anyone to do this, with this Grade I listed building, the only enclosed dock space left in Britain, we should ask ourselves what sort of a Civic Society and city were we. Today we have the Albert Dock we hoped for but, I do remember, standing on the side of the dock with these derelict buildings, where it was all mud. The Mersey Docks and Harbour Board had let the water out

Paula Ridley, Lady President of the Students' Union at Liverpool University in 1964.

because they said the water regime was too expensive to maintain. The chairman of the city planning committee told a Granada Television crew, 'Mrs Ridley thinks this could be a tourist attraction, I ask you?' I wish I had that clip now.

Over the years I have worked all over the country in connection with matters of regeneration and urban development but my interest in Liverpool is paramount. As far as our architectural heritage is concerned we have on the waterfront, the three most important buildings which say 'Liverpool': the Liver Building, the Cunard Building and the Mersey Docks and Harbour Board Building. If you showed a photograph of them to anyone almost anywhere in the world they would instantly know this as Liverpool's seafront. Many towns and cities would kill for that instant recognition. They are amazing civic monuments to what was at one time, a very confident city.

We don't look after our buildings in Liverpool even now. Of course they cost a lot of money to maintain and this is not a city with a lot of money. It took a long time for people to realise that it was an advantage to hang on to our Georgian terraces – we have more Georgian houses than Bath – and not demolish them.

I do think now there is recognition and understanding of the importance of our built environment but we are still very casual about it. The city aspires to be European City of Culture in 2008 so we should not be allowing the Garden Festival Hall to fall into disrepair and we should have found a

more sensitive way to deal with the old, Liverpool airport, the only Grade I, thirties airport left in the country, with its two original wings, signifying flight, obscured by new development.

I was on the board of the Merseyside Development Corporation until its demise in 1998 and have always been interested in urban regeneration and what makes places tick. One day I got a call from a government department saying they were going to set up this organisation that would take over all the high rise tower blocks in Liverpool. Would I like to be the chairman? I could see my whole life changing before my eyes but I agreed and was appointed chairman of what became Liverpool Housing Action Trust – known as HAT. It's been a very interesting exercise. We began with five temporary seconded people and a year later we had 150 staff and owned sixty-seven tower blocks. Our job is to manage them, re-develop them

A visit to Liverpool Playhouse for Paula Ridley (right) with her husband, Professor Frederick Ridley.

Paula Ridley with one of the since destroyed blocks of high rise flats, 1993.

and look after the tenants, most of whom today are elderly.

In the 1960s when people were being moved out from the inner city, tower blocks were regarded as THE place to live. At the time people thought it was going to be Nirvana, cheap, using land in a very tidy way. Remember that those in the back-to-back houses of areas like Everton were living in very poor conditions. So, I can see that the civic leaders of the time thought they were doing everyone a favour. But the time will come when there will be very few of these blocks left apart from those round Sefton Park and Woolton. As the population of Liverpool is declining, so dramatically, we do not need the five and half thousands units we have in tower blocks. Originally

over a hundred were built but, we have already demolished quite a few and there are only forty-four left. We are replacing them with houses on the ground.

There have been many changes in Liverpool over the years I have been here, but I hope we have shaken off the impression other parts of the country had of us. It took us a long time to rid ourselves of the image we had in the 1980s. When I was in London on business then I would be asked how things were in Liverpool and you did begin to think you were being corralled up.

But I don't think people are frightened of Liverpool now. They come here for weekends, the hotels are full. Places like Liverpool's Tate Gallery, have helped to put together a package to present to the outside world that shows this is a serious place. After all, the Tate came to Liverpool with contemporary work because the Walker Art Gallery was so wonderful and had all those marvellous, particularly nineteenth-century pieces, and the Tate complemented it very nicely.

I think it is wrong to say that Liverpool is a city which is divided class-wise. The real problem is that the middle classes do not live in Liverpool. They tend to live out in the Wirral or up the line towards Formby and Freshfield. That has done a lot of damage; people come into the city to work then go home to somewhere quite different, where they have their own cinemas and restaurants. A different life.

Another interesting thing is the way that the business community has withdrawn from local politics in Liverpool. Funnily enough my thesis for my MA in 1970 was on this subject. In the 1930s, 40s and 50s they played a very political role in things; I actually mapped out the establishment links that there were. They all sat on each others boards so there was a very clear Establishment who moved in the same circles. I doubt if that is so today. There are people whose families have been here a long time; people who have put a huge amount into the city for absolutely nothing. I know most of them and they know me but I don't ever consider myself part of an Establishment and I don't think they would either. That world has moved on.

The key to Liverpool is its future. We hear all these plans: the Liverpool Vision, shopping here, shopping there. I personally am a bit cynical about them because to have all that sort of dramatic spending and getting, you have to have an economic motor for the city, to sustain it. We still have not cracked that entirely.

Paula Ridley (b.1944) is chairman of the Liverpool Housing Action Trust, chairman of the Victoria and Albert Museum in London and the director of the Calouste Gulbenkian Foundation (UK Branch). She lives in Liverpool with her husband Professor Frederick Ridley.

CHAPTER 16
Brian Labone

Brian Labone, Everton Captain celebrates his team's win over Sheffield Wednesday in the 1966 Cup Final.

Football was always an important thing in my life, from the time I was a small boy. My father, who was a keen Evertonian, used to take me to the match and I'd watch the game sitting on his shoulders. When I was eight or nine I went in the boys' pen which cost fourpence, in old money.

There were vast crowds in those days with gates of between 60,000 and 70,000. Apart from Manchester United where they get 60,000 fans now, football does not attract such big crowds today. The capacity at Anfield and Goodison is more like 40,000. This is due not only to the fact that there is less standing room but because people have other things to do with their leisure time. When I was growing up, football was the working mans' recreation. But there is no doubt that as a city, Liverpool is more fanatical about football than most places – whether you are an Everton or a Liverpool supporter. You've got whole families who have split loyalties: some go to Anfield, some to Goodison.

I always knew which side I was on: Everton. As a small boy, I wore a blue and white scarf for the match and carried a rattle. Rattles are now banned but, in those days it did not seem right to go to a football match, if you did not take a rattle.

My family lived in Norris Green when I was born, then we went posh and moved to Walton and finally Lydiate.

Liverpool Collegiate to which I had won a scholarship was more a rugby than a football school but I did play for Merseyside Grammar Schools and when I was at Belfield, Everton's training ground, someone spotted me and asked if I wanted

to play for them. I was seventeen and the idea of becoming a professional footballer had more appeal than going to university. It was 1957 and I signed for Everton and played for them right through until 1972 when an injury to my Achilles tendon put paid to my career. I was thirty-two and it was a blow, but Harry Catterick, the Manager, was very understanding. 'Look on the bright side, Brian, he said. If you'd been a horse we'd have shot you.'

My first wage packet was £7 a week and I got a £20 signing fee which my old man snaffled. When my football career finished in 1972 I was earning £150 a week. I was eighteen when I got into the first team where I stayed for virtually the rest of my career. When I started, there was a certain glamour about being a top footballer, even then, though nothing like it is today. You'd actually see Everton – and Liverpool – players walking through town. Now they whizz away in their limousines and head off for their haciendas or wherever they live.

In 1964, when I was made captain of Everton it was a big honour. I was captain until 1971 and they were wonderful years. We won the FA Cup in 1966 against Sheffield, 3-2. We also won the League Championship in 1962-63, were Cup Finalists in 1968 and League Champions in 1969-70. Additionally I had twenty six England caps from 1962 to 1970.

To win the Cup and a couple of championships in ten years was not bad but Liverpool eclipsed us and now you have Man United winning the League every year.

When John Moores took over Everton in

the 1960s we became known as the Millionaire-oes, because he was a millionaire. It meant Everton could go out and buy a player for £30,000 which today sounds ludicrous. But forty years ago it was a lot of money. During training, John Moores was not above putting on a pair of flying boots, tucking his trousers into them and demonstrating how he thought a player should run down the left wing.

Harry Catterick, was Everton manager when Bill Shankley was manager at Liverpool. Catterick was more autocratic than Shanks, though despite the intense rivalry between the clubs they were great friends. But there is no doubt that the rivalry never abates. There are Evertonians who will not eat tomatoes because they are red and Liverpudlians who would never

dream of buying a blue car – even if it was the only one available.

Originally the rivalry stemmed from religion because Everton drew most of their players from Eire, which meant they were Catholic. When I started playing for Everton people thought I was a Catholic. In fact though my mother was an Irish Catholic I was brought up C. of E., because my Dad was C. of E., so I was only half Catholic.

After my mother died nine years ago, I was told that while my father had been away in the army, she had whipped me down to the Catholic Church and had some sort of ceremony performed where I was almost christened a Catholic. I don't know whether that was hearsay but I have found

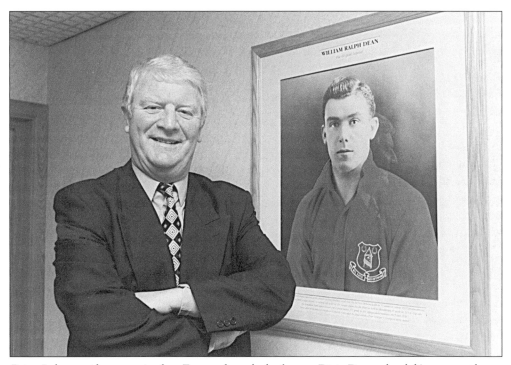

Brian Labone with a portrait of an Everton legend, the famous Dixie Dean, the club's greatest player.

Up and over: Brian Labone heads the ball in an international against Northern Ireland in 1969.

a certificate which showed I had been made a member of some Catholic Society.

Leading Everton out onto the pitch at Goodison with between 60,000 and 70,000 fans cheering you on, was a marvellous experience. Going down the tunnel and onto the Wembley pitch when Everton was in the Cup Final was more stressful. Your guts were churning, it was like going to the dentist.

To lose in the Cup Final is terrible but to win absolutely wonderful. When we lifted the cup in 1966, Princess Margaret presented it to me. Then she was still very beautiful; a real cracker. The Royals must have blue blood because I could see the veins on her thin little hands. They were blue.

One thing in which Liverpool and Everton fans are as one is in their hatred of Manchester United. But Liverpool fans probably hate Man United more than Everton do. This is because they think Man United have stolen Liverpool's rightful position as number one in the league and holder of the cup.

Bill Kenwright's control at Everton has given the club stability. Bill has a reputation as a good businessman but there is still a bit of the schoolboy about him. His love for Everton borders on obsession but it is a nice sort of insanity. He comes up to Liverpool for every match. He's a bit like the Pied Piper giving out tickets to the kids. Though it is a long time since I played for Everton I'm still involved. I handle the PR on match days.

Liverpool as a city I love. There is only one thing wrong with it – the name. It should be called Everton!

Brian Labone (b. 1940) was captain of Everton Football Club from 1964 to 1971. He lives in Lydiate.

CHAPTER 17
Linda Grant

Linda Grant, novelist and journalist.

Linda's parents Benny and Rose Grant.

Though I was born and grew up in Liverpool, both my mother and father were from immigrant families, part of the Jewish community who settled in the city at the beginning of the twentieth century. My father's family were from Poland, where there had been a big pogrom in 1903. After that, many Poles left to go to America. But some were 'done' on their tickets and though they thought they were *en route* to the United States, they only came as far as Liverpool. My father's family was among them, though he was only six months old at the time. His father – my grandfather – set up as a baker in Brownlow Hill. My mother's family were from Kiev, in the Ukraine. They met when she applied for a job at the hairdressing business my father ran, in London Road. He supplied hairdressing products to the trade, cold perms, shampoos, capes, those stand-up hair dryers. That was how he made his money.

From the time I was eight, we lived in Booker Avenue which was very suburban, five minutes walk from the synagogue and in the middle of the Jewish community. There were around 6,000 Jews in Liverpool at the time my sister Michele and I were growing up: now I think there are only half that number. We had a very English childhood. My father's motto was, 'Only the best for my children.' So we went to private schools, first Beechenhurst Preparatory School in Menlove Avenue, then Belvedere, the G.P.D.S.T. school in Dingle. At Belvedere, the Jewish girls went off to a room on their own during assembly. But we could still hear the others singing *All Things Bright and Beautiful* so I grew up familiar with the sound of English hymns. When I was about thirteen I started skiving off school to go to lunchtime sessions at the Cavern. At sixteen I was hanging out with people like Adrian Henri, Roger McGough and Brian Patten – the Liverpool Poets – at the Philharmonic pub. They seemed terribly grown up and sophisticated, though they were only in their twenties. The idea that you could talk to them and they were famous, seemed incredible.

Going home from school I used to get off the bus two stops too early and stand outside Paul McCartney's home in Forthlin Road. One day it was so cold his father came out and invited me in for a cup of tea and a couple of digestive biscuits. He was very nice, but he was not Paul McCartney.

To be sixteen in Liverpool in 1967 was to be in the single most exciting place in the whole wide world, particularly if, like me, you wanted to be a writer. My parents desperately wished me to leave school at sixteen, go to Miss Foulkes Secretarial College, get a job with a firm of solicitors, marry one of them, have my first baby at twenty and live round the corner in Allerton.

The plan might have worked if I had not been in Liverpool but I was and the combination of being sent to Belvedere, which was a good school, and being part of the sixties scene meant that my parents' ambitions for me becoming a suburban housewife, were never going to go anywhere.

I left school just before my eighteenth birthday and went to work on the *Widnes Weekly News*, as a reporter. After a spell as Press Officer for Oxfam I took my A-levels at what was then Childwall Hall College of Further Education and is now the headquarters for Brookside. Then I read English at York University and though I keep coming back I have not lived properly in Liverpool since then. My mother never forgave me. She said she was the only mother whose daughter went away to university and never came back.

Even if I didn't, I have always been aware of the influence the city has had on me. I myself never experienced any anti-Semitic feeling in Liverpool. But it must have existed because in 1954, my father changed the family name from Ginsberg to Grant. He had received a threatening letter which was signed 'from an anti-Semite.' I still have that letter.

I remember the Liverpool Jewish community, when I was growing up, as very confident and thriving. Though there were no Hampstead type intellectuals about. They were businessmen: doctors, accountants, lawyers. Most of my friends' parents had not been born in Britain, had no education but built themselves up from nothing.

Our house was a straight down the middle Jewish home. Kosher food, the ritual of the candles, chicken soup and roast chicken every Friday night. I'd never seen

Linda with her mother.

a pork chop until I was at the home of a non-Jewish friend. I ate it – but I did not tell my mother.

There were plenty of Kosher food shops where she shopped. My father was a member of the Jewish Golf Club. He went to the Synagogue on Saturday morning though it was nothing to do with being religious. More of being involved with the Jewish community in terms of charity work and fund raising.

As my mother was something of a fashion plate I spent a large part of my childhood in Bold Street where the shops were wonderful. There was one called Cripps where they had a whole room of glass-fronted cabinets containing party dresses. If my mother bought a hat it came in a box. If she bought a dress, so did that. The last time I was in Liverpool, I noticed that the chair labelled the largest hearing aid in the world was still in the window of the hearing aid shop in Bold Street. As it had been for the whole of my childhood.

Like so many Liverpudlians I remember the special foodie smell of Coopers – the Fortnum and Masons of Liverpool. Andre Bernard, where my mother had her hair done twice a week.

But most of all, I remember the late 60s when Liverpool seemed like the capital of Britain. So much happened then. I was lucky to be there, though one thing has always struck me about Liverpool – how apart it seems, from the rest of England. It's certainly nothing to do with Lancashire and as for places like Widnes and Runcorn, they may be just a few miles up the road but they have a different accent and a different culture. It's probably something to do with it being a seaport and every city that is a seaport is different.

Linda Grant (b. 1951) is a feature writer for The Guardian. *Her first novel,* The Cast Iron Shore *won the David Higham First Novel Award and her second,* When I Lived in Modern Times, *the Orange Prize for Women's Fiction in 2000. Her family memoir,* Remind Me Who I Am Again *won the Mind Book of the Year. She lives in London.*

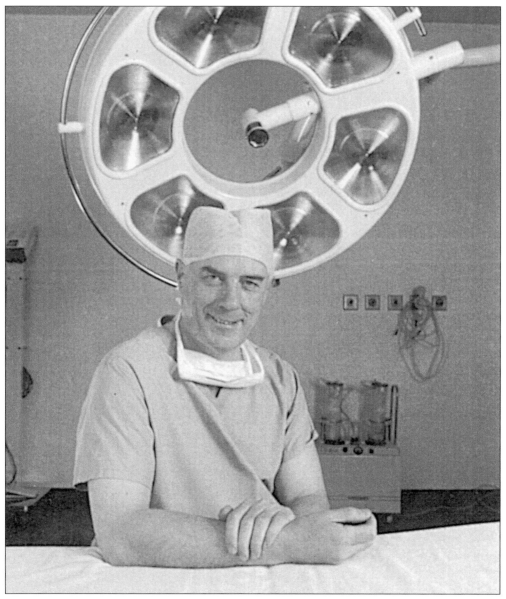

CHAPTER 18

Proffessor Ray Donnelly, founder and Vice President of the Roy Castle Lung Cancer Foundation.

Roy and Fiona Castle with Ray Donnelly, before the Train of Hope left Lime Street Station in 1994.

My first sight of Liverpool was on a cold, wet, rainy day in 1974. I was thirty-even and I had come to have a look both at the city and Broadgreen Hospital where, I was thinking of applying for the post of consultant in cardiao-thoracic surgery. At the time I was Senior Registrar at Leeds General Infirmary. That day I did not go into the city but I do remember visiting the Medical Institution and being very impressed. I thought how, one day, I would love to be able to speak there (eventually I did – several times!)

I did not know then how emotionally as well as professionally, my life would become bound up with Liverpool and I certainly had no idea that I would play a leading part in establishing in Liverpool the Roy Castle International Centre for Lung Cancer Research – the only lung cancer research institution in the world.

On that rainy day in 1974, I was more concerned with the idea of working in Liverpool which had always had a strong medical tradition, particularly in my specialist field, thoracic surgery. I was aware that there was a great deal of lung disease in the area and therefore much work to be done. The day I was appointed consultant at Broadgreen I thought that if I died tomorrow,then I could do so as a happy man, I'd achieved my ambition: I was a consultant.

My salary was £5,000 a year, which I thought wonderful and the house in Calderstones, into which my wife, Elizabeth and our five children moved cost £17,000.

The thing that struck me initially about working in Liverpool as opposed to Leeds was the difference in the patients. They were so much more open and trusting: they had a sense of humour and were easy to relate to. The first ward round I did at Broadgreen, it hit me in the eye, how different Liverpool people were and I liked them.

Though I was dealing in surgery in all its aspects within my field, including heart surgery at Myrtle Street Children's Hospital, I became increasingly concerned about the amount of lung cancer around. Sometimes I would see ten or twelve new cases in my various clinics, including the Isle of Man.

In the late 1980's Sam Watkins, one of our registrars at Broadgreen produced a paper which showed that something like 2,000 people a year were developing lung cancer in the Greater Merseyside area and that only five per cent of them would survive five years. The figures were shocking and really focussed my mind and made me decide that we must get a research programme going in Liverpool. As I saw it, we not only had a great opportunity but also a great responsibility to do this.

Though everyone was enthusiastic there was no money available, either in the University or the Health Authority or the major charities I approached; so I thought I'll do it myself. On 18 April, 1990 I called my secretary, Sheila Christian and one of my patients, Eric Morris, into my office and we had our first meeting. I set out my ideas and objectives and these are the same now as they were then. To make people aware of the seriousness of the problem and to develop an intense programme of research into the cause, prevention and management of lung cancer.

We made ourselves the first three trustees and the Lung Cancer Fund was born. Early the following year we attained charitable status and over 200 attended when the Lung Cancer Fund was launched publicly by Ken Dodd and Libor Peseck, then conductor at the Liverpool Phil'. The first thing we did was to appoint a specialist lung cancer nurse to counsel patients. What used to happen was that I would sit in my clinic with the patient opposite and no matter how kindly or sympathetically you spoke to them, the minute you mentioned the words 'lung cancer' you could see the eyes glaze over; they would often be shocked and tearful. Then they would have to go out through the general outpatients department, often with a handkerchief to their eyes, and catch the bus home. The idea of the nurse was that she took them into a specially equipped room, comforted them, gave them a cup of tea and her telephone number so that they ring her with any questions or problems. She would also be there to see them when they went into hospital for investigations and operation.

The news that they have lung cancer – any cancer come to that – is a terrible shock to anyone. One of the most distressing things about it is that you do not need to have been a smoker yourself to contract it. Roy Castle did not smoke and neither did Derek Worlock, the Archbishop of Liverpool who was a patient of mine. I remember the Saturday morning I removed his lung, very well. I was aware that if anything went wrong, I, as the surgeon, would be under the spotlight. In fact the Archbishop made a reasonable recovery and lived for a few years more. He was a good patient but found the chemotherapy, which followed the operation difficult.

Cliff Richard with Ray Donnelly and Fiona Castle when Cliff opened the Roy Castle Lung Foundation in 1997.

When in 1993 I finalised my plans for a unique, international research centre for lung cancer in Liverpool, we asked Roy if he would give his name to the £12m appeal to build, equip and run it. He said, 'You can use my name but I can't do much for you because I am not very well.' Well, what he did was quite extraordinary. The Roy Castle Cause for Hope Appeal was launched at St George's Hall in Liverpool in January, 1994. Despite the fact that he was very ill and had only a few months to live, Roy insisted on travelling on the Train of Hope which spent three days going round the country raising funds. He died shortly afterwards.

Roy did not live to see the research centre in London Road which was named after him, and which was opened by Cliff Richard in 1997 but I am sure he would be delighted with what we are doing. The centre is a tribute to the people of Liverpool as much as anything else. They took us to their hearts in a fantastic way from the very beginning in 1990. I have said many times and seriously believe that I do not think this charity would have taken off anywhere else in the country, the way it did on Merseyside. It would have been much harder anywhere else.

By the time Roy Castle became associated with our fundraising we had already raised several hundred thousand pounds towards our goal. In 1992, Nicola Lawrence a beautiful twenty-five years old air stewardess from Aughton became one of my patients. Though she had never smoked, she had lung cancer and lived for only four months after she was diagnosed. In that time she, her family and friends, raised over £100,000 for the Lung Cancer Fund and we arranged for her to go and see Roy Castle.

It was about the time he had been diagnosed as having lung cancer and she asked him if he would help her with what was called the Nicola Lawrence Appeal. He agreed and came to Liverpool to launch a poster campaign for the Lung Cancer Fund. Afterwards I took him to meet the patients at the Cardio-thoracic Centre at Broadgreen and, although he wasn't well and had travelled a long way, he was great with everyone and cheered them up. .

Professor Ray Donnelly (b. 1936) retired from surgical practice in 1997 to concentrate on the Foundation. He is Proffessor of Lung Cancer Studies at Liverpool University and lives in Liverpool.

CHAPTER 19
Ian Tracy

Ian Tracey – a very young Organ Scholar.

Though Liverpool, as a whole, is very close to my heart, the Anglican Cathedral where I have been organist for the last twenty years is particularly important. It is a tremendous, magnificent building. I never enter it without a feeling of awe and being aware of the privilege of making music there on a daily basis.

John Betjeman famously said that in Liverpool Cathedral suddenly one sees the art of architecture that lifts one up and turns one into a king, yet compels reverence, is the art of enclosing space. And that is what Giles Gilbert Scott, the architect knew about.

Apart from the religious significance, the Cathedral is a wonderful place for grand occasions because we have the space and the know-how. Much of the latter goes back to the first Dean, Dean Dwelly. He was Dean from 1931 to 1955 and had a real sense of theatre. We are still doing the things he began all those years ago.

Who can forget the poignancy of the Hillsborough service in 1989 which was televised and went round the world. Normally it takes us months to get a service like that on the road – but we did it in ten days.

Then there was the drama of the Pope's visit in 1982. As he was Polish and knowing that his first name was Karol I thought it would be a bit kitsch to adapt a Polish carol for the choir to sing, in Polish. At the time we had a Polish student and he helped with translation and pronunciation. The Pope got the joke because he turned to David Sheppard, then Bishop of Liverpool and said, 'Aah! Chreestmas!'

The Queen came to open the Cathedral when it was completed in 1978. I was Assistant Organist then and she was interested in the technology involved in the service. Some years later at a Buckingham Palace garden party, she asked me if I was still at the Cathedral. I said, 'I am amazed you remember that, Ma'am.' She replied 'Well, you were very young and one has only opened one Cathedral in one's reign.'

When Princess Diana came in 1995 she had heard about the white socks, I always wear when I am playing the organ. It enables me to see where my feet are on the pedals and I've got hundreds of pairs. She asked if she could see them – so I hoisted up my cassock and showed her.

When I became organist, in 1980, I was twenty-five, the youngest Cathedral organist in the country. Before that Noel Rawsthorne, was the organist and I had been his Organ Scholar and later his assistant. Noel took over from the famous Goss Custard, who was Cathedral Organist for thirty-eight years, from 1917 to 1955. They were hard acts to follow.

Music was in my blood right from the time I was born in West Derby. My grandfather played the piano and organ, my grandmother the piano and my mother the piano, violin and piano accordion. There were various military bandmasters in the family. One of my first musical memories is being taken to a concert at the Liverpool Phil', by my father when I was five. Charles Groves was the conductor and it was an ideal concert for a youngster: Benjamin Britten's *Young Person's Guide to the Orchestra*, Grieg's *Piano Concerto* and Dvorak's *New World Symphony*.

We did not have a piano at home but my Nana lived round the corner and I used to spend hours in her front room practising. When I was five or six, I joined the choir at St Paul's Church, Derby Lane in Stoneycroft. The organist started giving me lessons and when I went on to Highfield School the Head of Music was Assistant Organist at the Cathedral. He used to take me to the Cathedral for organ lessons and eventually handed me on to Noel. By the time I was fifteen I had a set of keys to the Cathedral and knew how to lock up. That sort of thing could not happen now. It was often ten o'clock at night by the time I had finished practising, but I was never frightened being in the Cathedral on my own.

Liverpool Cathedral organ is world famous. It is mentioned in just about every book that has been written about organs, because it was the largest musical instrument ever constructed when it was built, in the 1920s.

There could never be another one like it because there would just not be the money. It is insured for four and a half million pounds – the Cathedral itself is only insured for eight and a half million.

One of my jobs is to oversee its maintenance. Its rather like the Forth Bridge: by the time you've finished at one end its time to start at the other. It has to be tuned fifty days a year. At the moment we are re-furbishing the keys; they are seventy-four years old and have got a bit clicky and clacky.

Liverpool has another famous organ – the one at St George's Hall. It is the third largest in the country and, as Organist to the City of Liverpool, I play there and make sure that it is properly maintained as well.

The Cathedral also has a very long and very fine choral tradition. We have thirty-two choristers but only twenty-four of them sing

The Queen talks to Ian Tracey as she openes the completed Anglican Cathedral in 1978.

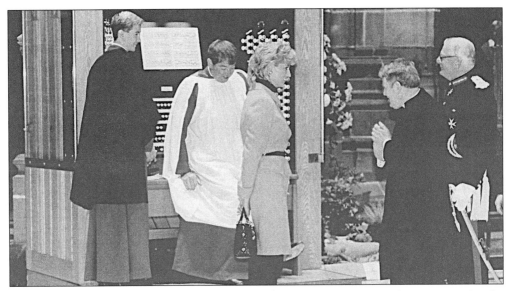

Ian Tracey steps down from the organ at Liverpool Cathedral which Diana, the late Princess of Wales visited in 1995 on her last official engagement. Alan Waterworth, the Lord Lieutenant and Derrick Walters, the late Dean of Liverpool are also in the picture.

in the first 'team'. The rest are training. They have to work hard because they are at the Cathedral six days week. There is a rehearsal most days at four o'clock; they are here all day Sunday and half day on Saturday.

Then there is the Liverpool Philharmonic Choir, now considered one of the finest in the country. Fortunately it is only ten minutes walk from the Cathedral, so commuting is not a problem for me.

My own favourite time at the Cathedral is Easter, but Christmas is particularly busy. We have twenty or so carol services at the Cathedral, eight at the Philharmonic and three at St George's Hall. So, by the time you get to Christmas you are completely saturated with carols. Whereas at Easter, with six weeks penitential music, there is a glorious transformation on Easter Day.

There are, of course, times when things go wrong. One Civic Sunday I sounded the fanfare for the Lord Mayor's entrance at the appointed time of 10.28 am and he had not arrived. He had mistaken the time and was sitting in his coach in Rodney Street, having a cigarette and killing half an hour. He had to shuffle in down the side, when the service had begun, instead of processing down the aisle.

Professor Ian Tracey (b. 1955) was appointed Organist at Liverpool Cathedral in 1980. He is also Organist to the City of Liverpool, at St George's Hall, Chorus Master of the Royal Liverpool Philharmonic Orchestra and Fellow and Organist at Liverpool John Moores University. He lives in Liverpool.

CHAPTER 20

Sir Trevor Jones

Sir Trevor Jones – 'Jones the Vote'.

The fact that I went away to sea at the age of sixteen was nothing unusual. It was the natural thing to do. In those days there was hardly a family, in Liverpool who did not have someone at sea. All the men in my father's family were seamen. My Dad was only fourteen when he first went.

I joined the Blue Star line and on my first voyage I was away for eleven months. I remember my Dad met me at Huskisson Dock when I came home.

Our family were what you'd call 'Northenders': we lived in Litherland. So when I was going back off leave I'd get on the Overhead Railway which stopped at Seaforth, then walk the rest of the way, with my seabag over my shoulder. That was always a very lonely walk because you did not know how long you were going to be away.

When I finally came ashore in 1948, I was twenty-two. I went to work with my Dad on the docks where he was a gig boatman helping manoeuvre ships in and out of the docks. In twelve years we built up a successful business and I wore out two bikes cycling up and down the Dock Road. It was hard going over the cobbles.

Then the docks were very busy. Sometimes as many as eighteen ships docked in one day. Every berth would be full. There were two Guinness boats a day carrying massive barrels of Guinness. You would see huge, five hundred pound bales of cotton being unloaded and wonder how anyone could lift them onto the trolleys. There was a knack in it. It was a tough life on the docks because you worked according to the tides and against the elements. When the north-west wind was blowing it was perishing. I'd get on my bike in my oilskins, but underneath I'd have sheets of brown paper to keep the wind out. Where possible you took advantage of shelter from the Overhead Railway – the Docker's Umbrella.

Eventually I went into business as a ships' chandler and Doreen, my wife came in to do the office work, which meant she had to learn to type. She was a beautician by training.

My participation in local politics began when a woman carrying a clip board arrived in my office and asked where I would like the business to be re-located. It was 1963 and the first I had heard of the Liverpool City Re-Development Plan. It was a matter of compulsory purchase orders being made to make way for these re-developments. The people of Liverpool had not been consulted but treated with contempt. The battle was on and I got involved. Everyone was against it. When Bessie Braddock's husband John, the Labour leader on the City Council, dropped dead on the steps of the Walker Art Gallery, he had just been to see the model of the city's re-development and thought it was too much to ask in human terms. He was on his way to the Bluecoat Chambers, to see Graeme Shankland, the architect, and tell him so.

When it was all over and the fight had been taken to the House of Lords – among other places – Lord McAndrew, who had been Chairman of Ways and Means under Churchill invited me to lunch and told me that if things were so bad in Liverpool I should do something about it. He said there were two ways of changing our society: the first was by revolution, but the British were

Trevor Jones in action in Liverpool City Chamber.

not much given to that; the second was through the political system, becoming part of it and bringing about change. He told me to get the manifestoes of the different political parties and join the one which most resembled the sort of society I wanted to live in.

I became a Liberal, though in 1968 when I was elected to the City Council, I was only the second councillor of that party. By 1973 we had forty-eight Liberal councillors and an overall majority. In 1971 I became National President of the Liberals and acquired the nickname 'Jones the Vote.' By this time, my wife Doreen, was also on the City Council, so we were a political family. She eventually became Lord Mayor, though

not before there had been a lot of dirty dealing and voting to keep her out.

That was the way of things. I have always said that Liverpool Council Chamber is a pit of despair. No quarter is asked or given. Its rough and its tough but the Liberals succeeded by being rougher and tougher than others; though we did it with a smile on our face.

The Militant years were hard. It got to the point where council officers were scared to be seen talking to me. If I stopped to speak to them outside the Municipal Annexe they'd be edging round the corner in case Derek Hatton, Tony Mulhearn and Tony Byrne were around. The day they came into power they got a screw driver and ripped the name off the door of the office I had occupied as Leader off the Council, then ransacked the place.

I watched their progress with interest because I knew the way they were going, they would not be able to balance the books. Unfortunately, Mike Reddington, the City Treasurer did not stand up to them. The District Auditor stepped in and the surcharge on the rates came about. It was an absolute reign of terror. Committee meetings lasted five minutes, there was no debate, everything was steamrollered through, by the Militants.

In local politics – as elsewhere – you need a gut instinct for the political process. Mrs Thatcher had it, whether you liked her or loathed her. In the aftermath of the Toxteth Riots in 1981, I got a call from Downing Street saying that she would be visiting the city next day. I advised her PA that the situation was still too tender. Three days later, the phone rang at five o'clock in the morning. It was her PA again to say that she had just left Downing Street on her way to Liverpool and would I make all the security arrangements. I got the Chief Constable Ken Oxford, out of bed.

There was a meeting at the Town hall before she left to drive back to London. Doreen, who was Lord Mayor, asked John Pearce, the manager at the Adelphi, to prepare some sandwiches for her and Dennis to have on the journey. He put a little bottle of wine in. On the Town Hall steps she said 'Sir Trevor. You have my private line. Please ring me any time you feel the need; but do remember, that I do not like being told I cannot go anywhere. Next day there was a letter of thanks for the sandwiches and a P.S., 'The wine was delicious.'

Sir Trevor Jones (b.1927) was knighted in 1981. He was Leader of the Liberals on Liverpool City Council from 1981 to 1983 and National President of the Liberal Party from 1972 to 1973. He lives in Liverpool.

CHAPTER 21
Derek Hatton

Derek Hatton, politician and broadcaster.

Shall I be a footballer and play for Everton or go into politics. A very small Derek Hatton ponders his future.

When I was a child, Liverpool was still a matriarchal society. Women ruled the roost; the men went out and earned the money but their wives managed everything. My mother, Alma, was no exception. She was only five feet nothing but she was an absolute powerhouse. When she told my Dad to jump he said 'How high?' She died in 1995 – it knocked the stuffing out of me. She was behind me in everything I did. During the Militant years she'd pick up the newspaper and say 'What's all this about?' I'd explain it to her and she would understand.

My interest in local politics began when I joined Liverpool Fire Brigade when I was seventeen. My Dad had been a fireman. For some strange reason I'd been through a period of being religious and got involved with youth club work at Childwall parish church. Believe it or not, I even sang in the choir. It did not last long – about two to three years. Then I thought Christianity was the answer to everything; now I am a confirmed and total atheist. When I joined the Fire Brigade I started seeing conditions which were appalling and I knew could not be right. One occasion which sticks in my mind was going to a chimney fire at a big old house in Bedford Street South, around 1968. There were fifteen Irish people living in one room, on the top floor and, in the corner, was a large mound of human excretia.

Apart from playing football I'd not made much of a mark at Liverpool Institute: I'd passed the scholarship to get in. But later, I did my O-levels and my A-levels and went down to London to study Community Development at Goldsmiths College.

I had not long married my wife, Shirley. She wasn't exactly a conventional bride. She wore a trouser suit rather than a traditional wedding dress and one of the guests of honour was Flash, the mongrel owned by Shirley's sister Pam. He sat at the back of the church and is in all the wedding pictures proudly wearing his white satin bow.

While I was in London, my interest in politics increased: I got involved with the squatters movement, anti-Fascist organisations and all the anti-Vietnam stuff. All the things that concern you as a student. Once I was back in Liverpool I immersed myself in community matters and the Labour Party. The rest, as they say, is history. I have no regrets about the years I spent on Liverpool City Council, or what we tried to do as Militants. Militant Tendency was only the name for a group of people within the Labour movement who believed basically in a Socialist Society, where power would go from one to the other. In the 1980s there was still a chance of doing this.

Yes, we were very far to the left; we believed it was the only way forward for the future. We wanted to change things. When we seized power in 1983, we had a definite plan. It was about housing, sports centres, job creation; about making sure we did not put up rents or rates. Five thousand homes were built in three and a half years, more than twice the number of every other city in the country put together.

The situation in Liverpool during the Militant years polarised everything. People either wanted to kiss the face off you or stab you in the back. Luckily most people wanted to kiss the face off you – which was why we kept winning elections. Even at the end, when we were chucked out, it was the House of Lords who had to remove us. We never lost an election in the city. People ask me if I had my time over again would I do the same. My answer is that if it was May, 1983 again, I would not do a single thing differently. If it was May, 2000, I would not do a single thing the same. This is because everything has changed: politics has changed, Derek Hatton has changed. In Liverpool, as elsewhere, society, thanks to Mrs Thatcher, is fundamentally different. Trade Unionism has virtually been wiped off the scene.

It makes me laugh when you get people who are still on the left who think they can effect changes. If we could not do it in the 80s with all the power, influence and support around, how are they going to do it now?

What caused our downfall was the structure of the national Labour Party. It was not simply Neil Kinnock: he was just its personification. Had we and other local authorities, of like mind, been given the support we were asking for, I think we would have seen a very different situation as far as the power of local government is concerned. And, Liverpool, like everywhere else would have benefited.

Today people say that Liverpool is improving and yes it is. But what happens the moment we get a little hiccup. We are very dependent on two things – the student population and tourism.

Liverpool, as everyone says, is unique. Its great on nicknames, which is why people call me Degsy still. It's got a natural

Derek Hatton, as a small boy, with his mother Alma, always his greatest fan.

Derek Hatton and his wife Shirley on their wedding day – Flash, the family pet came too.

aggression that has nothing to do with violence, but it's a different place from the city in which I grew up. When I was two and a half we went to live in a new housing estate in Childwall Valley. It was 1950 and it was great because there were a lot of other families with children of my age.

In my first year at Liverpool Institute, Peter Sissons was head boy. He seemed very straight laced to an eleven year old: a bit like a mini master. Paul McCartney was also there and was a hero because we used to go and hear him playing at the Cavern. When the school play was *The Merchant of Venice*, Bill Kenwright was Shylock and Steve Norris, Portia. By accident I got the part of Gratiano and when, at sixteen, I was

leaving, Kenwright asked me if I wanted to tour West Germany with the National Youth Theatre. My mother would not let me go. She had arranged for me to start work at Plessey's electrical engineering works and left me no doubt that this was where my future lay. In those days, sixteen year old Liverpool boys, did what their mothers told them!

Derek Hatton (b. 1948). Broadcaster, Member of Liverpool City Council from 1979 to 1987 and Deputy Leader from 1983 to 1987. He lives in Liverpool and London.

CHAPTER 22
Sir Richard Foster

Sir Richard Foster, Director of National Museums and Galleries on Merseyside.

Sir Richard Foster (left) with Andrew Durham when Liverpool's Conservation Centre was European Museum of the Year in 1998.

Culturally Liverpool has a tremendous amount going for it: famous pictures, wonderful museums, superb architecture and, overall a tremendous feeling of 'place.' The look of Liverpool is one of its greatest assets. It contributes more than anything to its cultural identity. But, sometimes I wonder if people, realise how many treasures we have here or how much is going on. Do they know what marvellous paintings we have in the Walker Art Gallery, for example: the Rembrandt self-portrait. Henry VIII by a follower of Hans Holbein and of course the famous 'And When Did You Last See Your Father?' by William

Yeam, plus one of the few panel paintings by Simoni Martine in this country. We are often asked to loan pictures to galleries as far flung as Washington and Tokyo. So we share our heritage with the world.

Then there is the John Moores biennial contemporary art exhibition, a wonderful Liverpool institution that has been going for forty years, but still attracts about 2,000 entries. It is very popular with the public and the artist prize winners are either at the threshold of a distinguished career, or are helped by the exhibition, to achieve that.

In 1968 David Hockney, almost certainly kick-started his illustrious career through the John Moores exhibition – that famous first prize winner of 'Peter getting out of Nick's pool'.

As I come up to retirement I am delighted that we have managed to win a grant of £24 million from the Heritage Lottery for re-furbishment of the Walker Art Gallery and to double the size of the Liverpool Museum so that we shall be able to show galleries which have not been seen since before the war. I like to think it is still a time honoured custom for parents to take their children to the Liverpool Museum, to look at the exhibits. Generations of them have gazed in awe at the famous dinosaur skeleton and the collections from Ancient Egypt, Greece and Rome – and I hope always will.

But things have certainly changed since 1978, when I came to Liverpool as Director of Merseyside County Museum. Then my responsibilities were Liverpool Museum, Speke Hall, where we undertook a big repair programme, and starting up Croxteth Country Park. But I also received a clear instruction that I was to develop a Maritime Museum. I'd only been here a short time when I was told to prepare a report and select a site. The idea came from Sir Kenneth Thompson and the Conservative administration of Merseyside County Council where there was an all-party agreement that the waterfront should be developed, with a Maritime Museum by the river. In fact there had always been an aspiration to create a maritime museum for Liverpool, advocacy appearing in the local press a hundred years ago. In 1940, Robert Gladstone of the Gladstone family, left money to the city for that specific purpose.

To test the water and see if the public would be interested in such a thing, we opened, in 1979, the Pilotage Building, near Man Island, for a short season. It was very successful – 60,000 visitors were attracted. Obviously there was keen interest in the restoration of public access to the Liverpool waterfront. Coincidentally the Toxteth riots happened, Michael Heseltine, became Minister for Merseyside and the government started to take an interest in Merseyside which required massive investment to restore the South Docks which had been left to go tidal. Eventually the Urban Development Corporation grew into Merseyside Development Corporation and that was my opportunity. Here was an agency that could work in partnership with the County Council, to provide investment and carry out essential repairs to a block of warehouses known as the Albert Dock, which could be used to house the Maritime Museum.

The overall theme was Liverpool and its international maritime links. Liverpool was, after all, the gateway to the Empire in the nineteenth century. It still is a major seaport, while much of its history had a strong local resonance because so many people worked in the port, or had relatives who have done so.

So we set about our plans and the Maritime Museum opened in 1996. Later, the installation of the Transatlantic Slave Gallery was highly controversial in terms of its interpretation, but Liverpool merchants were involved with slavery from the beginning of the eighteenth century. It was an important thing for us to do and we did so with the help of Peter Moores who funded the gallery and the associated research programme.

An Egyptian mummy case on display at Liverpool Museum.

Peter Getting Out of Nick's Pool' – the painting which launched David Hockney's career when it won first prize in the John Moores Exhibition in 1968.

Emigration was another aspect of maritime history that we included from the start. The fact that so many people left Liverpool to make a life in the New World, was important locally and internationally. There was so much to say; the famous shipping lines like Bibbys and Holts and, later on, the part Liverpool played in the Battle of the Atlantic.

In the mid 1990's, we were able to attract the Customs and Excise Museum to become part of the Maritime Museum, which added a further dimension to a museum now attracting over 300,000 visitors a year. The seam of maritime history is far from exhausted. But it is important to remember that the Maritime Museum and other waterfront developments like the Albert Dock became a shop window for the new Liverpool that was to emerge after the turbulent political situation in the 1980s.

At the same time, we had our problems.

The abolition of the Metropolitan County Councils – Merseyside County Council among them – by Mrs Thatcher in 1986 brought great changes in my in role. The Walker Art Gallery, which had been administered by the County Council, plus all the museums that I was responsible for, were 'orphaned.' It was in the days of Derek Hatton, and Liverpool City Council was not exactly putting museums at the top of its priorities. But the government decided that they would take over the funding of any museums with collections of an outstanding nature, that were adversely affected by abolition. Merseyside was the only place to achieve this national status. We became known as the National Museums and Galleries on Merseyside, responsible eventually for eight different institutions: the Walker Art Gallery, Liverpool Museum, Lady Lever Art Gallery, Sudley House, Maritime Museum, Museum of Life, Customs and Excise National Musuem and the Conservation Centre. Fifteen years later, we are still going strong. Our latest development is the Conservation Centre in Whitechapel. We are administered by a board of trustees, receive government aid of £14 million a year, employ 500 staff and attract around one million visitors annually.

The Lottery fund has made a big difference to museums, in the 1990s. But, if you get lottery money, though it may be generous, you have to find twenty five per cent of the gross budget yourself. So, as the renovations at Liverpool Museum and the Walker Art Gallery will cost £34m and our lottery grant is £24 million it is my job to fill the £10m gap.

In the old days Museum Directors never had to face up to such a challenge – but it is a fact of life today. We are not short of local benefactors and sponsors like Professors Phil Redmond and Rex Makin – and Littlewoods, but I have to spread my net wider to find such large amounts of money. Objective One status has been helpful in securing European Regional Development Funding. However, it has been a tremendous privilege to be in charge of the museums and galleries of a great city like Liverpool. I have enjoyed the opportunity and the challenge of developing the eight museums at a watershed in Liverpool's history at time when it was struggling to find itself.

My successor can look forward to huge challenges in the next few years dominated by the need to further develop the museums and galleries for the social, economic welfare of the region in the context of Liverpool's 800th anniversary in 2007 and its bid for the European Capital of Culture in 2008.

Sir Richard Foster (b. 1941) is Director of National Museums and Galleries on Merseyside and was knighted in January 2000. He lives with his wife, Mary, in Wirral.

CHAPTER 23

Gerry Marsden

Gerry Marsden, Liverpudlian singer and songwriter.

My Dad used to play the ukulele and that is one of my first memories. We lived in the Dingle in Menzies Street in a terraced house. It was very friendly and we did the things older people now talk about nostalgically. Even borrowing milk, sugar and bread. There was a communal spirit. If you went to the local rag and bone merchant you could get money for almost anything: old shoes and coats: whatever. Actually I enjoyed lessons at Our Lady of Mount Carmel school, but music was special – always had been. If a teacher asked me to look after the music class I'd burst into song. I was in the school and church choir and knew all there was to know about pop music.

Physically I was not particularly robust but I had plenty of spirit, which was just as well. There was a scrap almost every day in the school playground. Dingle was not a place for strangers and even if you lived there you kept strictly to your own area. There were dozens of gangs and we learned to take care of ourselves. There was hardly any reason for the fights. Our Menzies Street mob would meet another gang from another street and there would be a few bloody noses and swollen mouths. It was part of growing up. Luckily these gangs called truce for certain things, like delivering papers. To earn money for records and guitar strings, I delivered the Liverpool Echo every afternoon after school. It was important to get permission from rival gangs to go into their territory. Even if you had been in a punch up a few days earlier, they would let you in.

My Dad had this ukulele which he had brought home from the ship he had been aboard when he had been torpedoed in the war. I played it all the time but, when I was twelve he gave me a wonderful present, my first guitar; it was a twenty-five pound Spanish acoustic with a cut-away so that you could get your hands further down the neck. I was made up. We could not afford lessons, so I transposed all my father's chords from the ukulele to the guitar, adding an extra two strings. Then I bought Bert Weedon's book *Learn to Play in a Day*, which influenced many kids like me. Later, when I had the chance to appear on the same stage as Bert Weedon I was able to tell him personally that it was his book that had helped me to learn to play. After leaving school, my first real job was at the Kardomah Tea factory in the centre of Liverpool. I helped to make tea chests and we used to stand and sing the songs of the day while we worked. Making tea chests for a living was ironic in view of how later, in my skiffle group, we'd put string on a broom handle, attach it to the tea chest, and use it as a double bass.

At some point my Dad, who worked as a railways clerk, thought it was time I got a job with a future so he got me a position as a railways van delivery boy. This was hard work because of the hours. Working most nights with my skiffle group, I did not get home until two o'clock in the morning and I had to be on the wagon at the railway depot at six o'clock. I was so tired the driver let me grab a sleep in the back of the van during deliveries.

My skiffle group consisted of my brother Fred, who cut the top out of a biscuit tin, with a can opener, got some parchment paper and put it in, then jammed the top on. Then he bought some brushes and became the drummer. My Dingle pals Tommy Ryan

Gerry Marsden on the Mersey.

and Dixie Dean joined us on washboard, Jimmy Tobin was on tea chest bass and Matty Summers was the other guitarist. Gerry Marsden's Skiffle Group, with my Dad as manager, was available for engagements.

There were literally hundreds of groups like ours forming. Over in Woolton, John Lennon had started one called The Quarry Men, but we did not know they would turn into anything special. Our group played the same circuit. By 1958, when I was sixteen and on the railways, the music scene in Liverpool was throbbing with hundreds of rock 'n' roll groups. My skiffle group was now known as Gerry and the Pacemakers. By then John Lennon's Quarry Men had gone through several names to become The Beatles. I was friendly with all the groups. We would bump into each other in a record shop

called Nems in the city centre. That was where I got to know Lennon and Paul McCartney. We were all doing the same thing enquiring about the new rock 'n' roll hits from the States by people like Chuck Berry, Bo Diddley and Jerry Lee Lewis.

All this puzzled the manager; a quietly spoken and well dressed man named Brian Epstein. At this stage, Brian knew nothing about our shows, though only a couple of hundred yards from his office was the Cavern Club in Mathew Street.

I became very friendly with the Beatles, Lennon, McCartney, George Harrison and their drummer Pete Best – but only off stage. On stage I saw them as our biggest threat and I simply wanted to bury them musically. Even then I saw that the front line of John and Paul were tremendously talented. I developed a special affinity with John Lennon. We had similar outlooks and the same sick sense of humour. He was brilliant and had a sharp mind. Whatever he did with the Beatles, even as a guitarist was different. I thought, even then, that Lennon and McCartney were unstoppable, like an express train that had to roar out of Liverpool.

After the Beatles, my group, Gerry and the Pacemakers were the second group to be signed up by Brian Epstein in what became his stable of recording stars from Liverpool. During the Sixties we were hardly out of the charts with three number ones in a row. 'How do You Do It?', 'I Like It' and 'You'll Never Walk Alone.' But 'Ferry Cross the Mersey' remains the one people particularly remember.

As a Liverpool lad I feel I owe everything to Brian Epstein. He brought the Beatles out into the fore and we realised we could make it into the business. We could earn money and do what we loved.

Gerry Marsden (b. 1942) songwriter, musician and entertainer. He and his wife Pauline, live in Wirral.

'Ferry Cross the Mersey', *with Gerry Marsden.*

CHAPTER 24
Allan Williams

Allan Williams, the man who gave the Beatles away.

Allan Williams (left) with Paul McCartney (centre) and George Harrison and Pete Best (to the right) at the British War Memorial in Hamburg in the early '60s.

It's a long story, but I'm known as the man who gave the Beatles away – in fact, those words will probably be on my tombstone!

I first came across them when I was running the Jacaranada Club in Slater Street. It was a coffee bar and I'd got the idea having seen similar places in Paris. In those days, when the last tram left Lime Street, the night was over.

The Bohemian set, Adrian Henri, Roger McGough, Brian Patten, Beryl Bainbridge used to hang out there. So did all the Liverpool groups but then I did not know that John Lennon had formed a group with Paul McCartney, George Harrison and Stuart Sutcliffe. I was putting on groups at the Liverpool Stadium and, one day, John Lennon asked me when I was going to do

something for them. I had them down as coffee bar layabouts, from the art school. Because the basement at the Jacaranda was empty in morning, I let the groups use it for rehearsals. The Beatles knew this and used to miss their lectures to come down and listen to the groups performing. Pick up points and learn .

The only work I gave them was when I had problems with the ladies' toilet; which I had to share with the sweet shop next door. There was a communal corridor. With the groups hanging round, girls were writing obscene graffiti on walls. These old dears from the sweet shop complained, quite rightly. Knowing these layabouts from the art school I asked them to do me a favour and re-decorate the ladies' toilet and obliterate the graffiti. The work they did in those days was

Picasso style, throwing paint on the walls. Frankly, I preferred the graffiti to the mess they made. They were a little bit above the average intelligence. It was nice to talk to them even though they did bum free coffees and bacon butties.

They wanted to be known as the Beatles right from the beginning but this was considered stupid by some. Finally it was settled that they would be known as the Silver Beetles, which they hated. Some people could not understand the name 'Beatles' but it was a play on words. They were a beat group.

I still ran the Jacaranda but I could see times were a-changing. Instead of coffee bars, licensed clubs were coming in. So I opened a club called the Blue Angel in Steel Street, only 4 mins away. It was the first piano bar and was a huge success. Larry Parnes rang me to say he was coming to Liverpool with Billy

Fury, one of his rock stars, and he wanted a Liverpool group to back him. I thought I'd throw the Beatles in at the deep end because they did seem to be progressing. They had Stuart Sutcliffe, who was John Lennon's mate, as bass player. He was a terrible player who could not even face the audience. He used to play with his back to them because he did not want people to see he could only play three chords.

Billy Fury liked the Beatles because they were vibrant but had spotted poor Stuart Sutcliffe could not play and said he would have to go. To my amazement John Lennon said 'No'. Other groups would have given their eye-teeth to get the job but even in those days, the Beatles had their own direction.

By this time their performance was rough but good. I sent them to Hamburg for three months and they worked seven nights a week. They were so poor they had no money

The Liverpool Poets, Roger McGough, Adrian Henri and Brian Patten. 1985, who used to gather at the Jacaranda Club.

to go. Paul McCartney still owes me £15 he borrowed to buy some clothes. We agreed I would pay all the expenses. I said 'OK' it's £10 a head and you pay me out of your earnings'; which they never did either. Half way we stopped at Arnhem. There is a famous photograph of the Beatles taken at the cenotaph where the words 'Their name liveth for ever more' can be seen. It referred, of course, to those who had died in the war but bearing in mind what happened to the Beatles, the picture is symbolic. A lot of people think that the Cavern made the Beatles but it wasn't; it was the Hamburg days. The first gig they played where Beatlemania kicked off was when Bob Wooller got them a job at Litherland Town hall. Then they never looked back.

If you had heard them before Hamburg you would not have said they were going to be a world phenomenon. But Hamburg was where they served their apprenticeship. People ask me if it had not been the Beatles who made such a mark in the world, would it have been another group. My answer to that is that no, it wouldn't. They were part of a social revolution which was taking place. They were a phenomenon. They were different. They wrote their own music.

The second time I sent them to Hamburg I had a row with John Lennon. Stuart Sutcliffe rang me and said Lennon was refusing to pay my commission. As a result I wrote them a nasty note saying that they appeared to be more than a little swollen headed and reminding them that when I first managed them nobody wanted to know them. They were known as 'that bum band'. As a licenced theatrical agent I told them, they'd never work again. I sacked them. That's how I came to be known as the man who gave the Beatles away.

Then Brian Epstein came on the scene and became their manager, but I don't think even he realised what heights they would reach. He made them get rid of their leather gear and put them in those collarless suits. This was when Ringo joined the group. For some reason they wanted to get rid of Pete Best The rest, of course, is history. We got on good terms again, eventually. Brian Epstein came into the Blue Angel, from where I had banned them, and asked if I would let the Beatles in. I said, O.K. tell them to come in next time they are around. He said they were outside waiting.

I would be lying if I said that as I watched their progress, I did not feel frustrated. The biggest moment of frustration was when they appeared on *Sunday Night at the Palladium* and John Lennon told the people in the orchestra stalls not to clap but rattle their jewellery. I thought to myself 'I simply do not believe this. I used to manage that group!' I picked up a cushion from the sofa and threw it at the screen. If I'd had a brick handy, I'd have thrown that as well. Today the Beatles are as popular with the new generations as they were with the old. They were a phenomenon, the like of which we will not see again. Groups, like Oasis, come and go but the Beatles were unique.

Some parochial people have never forgiven them for leaving Liverpool, but they had to go. They belonged to the world. We should be proud they started here, in Liverpool. I am

Allan Williams (b. 1930) Theatrical agent and impressario. He lives in Liverpool.

CHAPTER 25

Elizabeth Steel

Elizabeth Steel after being sworn in as a Circuit Judge by Lord McKay, the Lord Chancellor.

My family have been lawyers since 1900, when my grandfather Thomas Steel founded the family firm in Warrington, though our links with the legal world in Liverpool have always been strong.

One of my first memories of Liverpool is being taken to watch the proceedings in St George's Hall, where the courts were held then. I must have been about eleven and I was put in the Grand Jury Box in Court number two, in the care of a nice woman police officer. Years later when I was practising as a solicitor in Liverpool, in Dale Street, a police sergeant came up to me and said 'Were you the little Alice-in-Wonderland who visited St George's Hall all those years ago?' Apparently it was his wife who had looked after me.

There are plenty of lawyers in the family. My father Edward Steel followed in his father's footsteps and became a solicitor. He was called to the Bar in 1937 and appointed a County/Circuit Judge in 1958. In turn, my sister Heather and I followed him. Today Heather is a High Court Judge and I myself have been a Circuit Judge since 1991, though I never intended to go into law. I wanted to do drama. However, my parents threatened me that if I did not work harder for my A-levels they would have me articled as a solicitor. In a fit of bad temper I said 'O.K. you do that.'

Liverpool is a fine place to be a lawyer. There is a variety of work and some excellent practitioners on both sides of the profession, including a very good Bar.

Elizabeth Steel as a baby with three generations of her family: grandfather Tom Steel, father Edward and great grandfather, also Edward.

Elizabeth Steel (centre), when President of Liverpool Law Society (1989-1990) with four women partners of Liverpool solicitors, Cuff Roberts. Left to right: Chris Aitken, Trish Cottrell, Sue Roberts and Annette Griffiths.

I loved it from the beginning and have no regrets, which, I suppose, is understandable. It's in the blood and the sight of my father working away at his briefs at home was familiar from childhood. Though, as children, we were banned from his study. It was a place you simply did not wander into.

He himself read Law at Liverpool University and when he went to the Bar, Sir Hartley Shawcross, who eventually became Attorney General in Clement Attlee's government was his pupils' master. I also decided to read Law at Liverpool University and was there from 1955 to 1958. It was a very different world from today. There were just thirty-five in my year in the Faculty of Law and only four were women. These days just over fifty per cent of law students are women. So when I qualified, women lawyers were thin on the ground. The first time I went to a Law Society dinner there were five hundred guests – only three of whom

were women. Once in the early 1960s, when I was appearing at Crewe Magistrates Court, a woman police officer asked me if I had noticed how many policemen were coming into court. She said they wanted to have a look at me because it was the first time they had seen a woman advocate. When I was young, we women did not say we were solicitors, because if you did people seemed to take three steps back. I suppose it was because there were so few of us. If anyone asked me what I did, I said I worked in a solicitor's office.

We were treated very cautiously by our male superiors. Some men would tell you bluntly that you were not going to be given any advantages just because you were a woman. Though just now and again, my principal would say 'Go along to court and "do a Rosie"'. This was a reference to Rose Heilbron and meant doing a gentle, sympathetic and eloquent plea in mitigation to the magistrates. Rose Heilbron is easily the most famous woman lawyer Liverpool has produced, largely because of appearing in some flamboyant trials, like the Cameo Cinema murder case, she was the first to do so many things. She was the first woman Leader of the Northern Circuit for instance; in 1956 she was appointed the first woman Recorder (at Burnley) and in 1974 she became a High Court Judge in the family division. She had to fight for recognition and was a real trailblazer. Today life is different for women lawyers in Liverpool, as elsewhere, because we are now fully accepted. Though there are, in the upper echelons – senior partners in solicitors' firms, Heads of Chambers and judicial appointments – less women proportionately than men, it is only relatively recently that large numbers of women entered the profession. And, interestingly, to date, I am the only woman to have become President of Liverpool Law Society, a position I was honoured to occupy from 1989-1990.

As a Circuit Judge I deal with three kinds of legal work: Civil, Family and Crime but I do notice that there are more women than men who are family law barristers. So the perception that women are better suited to certain sorts of legal work is still there. One of the biggest changes in my time has been the approach to family law. When I am sitting, I do not wear a wig and gown, but a dark suit, because it is less intimidating. Children rarely appear in court but are dealt with by welfare officers who report their findings. In the whole of my time as a Circuit Judge I think I have only actually seen three children in family cases. One was

Elizabeth Steel relaxing with some canine chums.

amusing because it concerned a seven year old boy who was going to be allowed to live with his grandmother, whom he loved. However, he refused to accept this as gospel, unless he was told it in person by the judge. So, I summoned him to my room and gave him the good news, with which he turned to his grandmother and said 'That was a waste of time wasn't it?' It turned out he was disappointed that I did not look like his idea of a judge. So I put on my wig and gown – and he went away happy as Larry.

Along with a more tolerant attitude to women lawyers there have been all sorts of changes in the legal life of Liverpool. The opening of the very modern Queen Elizabeth II Law Courts in Derby Square for instance has made life so much easier. They may lack the Gothic charm and romance of St George's Hall but that place had a lot of drawbacks. In particular the coke fumes down in the basement where Queens Counsel had their conference rooms!

Elizabeth Steel (b. 1936), a Circuit Judge since 1991, was appointed a Recorder in 1989. She was a member of the Cripps Committee which reported on the way the law and administration should be changed to give equality to women, from 1967 to 1969 and a member of the Race Relations Board from 1970 to 1978. Married to Stuart Christie, a retired solicitor, she lives in Liverpool.

CHAPTER 26
Libor Pesek

Libor Pesek poses before Liverpool's Roman Catholic Church.

The most emotional part of my career was in Liverpool, where from 1987 to 1997 I was Chief Conductor of the Royal Liverpool Philharmonic Orchestra – or 'the Phil' as it is affectionately known. When I left I was glad it was not a complete goodbye. That would have been a wrench – so it was comforting to know that as Conductor Laureate I would be returning regularly. I loved Liverpool right from the beginning and I love it still. When I came here we did not know each other but my first impression was that the city was a picture of my soul. It is a disorganised city, subject to some decadance, which I feel in my soul as well. There are so many affinities between myself and this city and, of course, the people.

The Philharmonic audience is tremendously loyal. For instance, when the Philharmonic Hall was being renovated and we performed for quite a long time, at the Anglican Cathedral, they faithfully followed us there, proving that they are ours and we are theirs. Both the orchestra and the management were surprised – and touched – at the way they showed their commitment. On the other hand, the Phil audience is not necessarily reflective of the whole of Liverpool. They are the people who have made it to a comfortable position in life. Not all of them are rich but they have enough money to be able to enjoy the arts.

My first visit to Liverpool was in 1986 when I was invited as a guest conductor. As it happened they were looking for a new conductor and at the end of the week, I was asked if I would be interested in applying for the job. I said that I wanted to stay at home

Libor Pesek conducting.

Libor Pesek (centre) with David Owen, Chancellor of Liverpool University and Philip Love, Vice Chancellor.

in Prague, the capital of the Czech Republic, though it was still under the boot of Communism. My manager said that Liverpool was not a backwater. It was a very important orchestra and if would be a good career move. So, I had a re-think. My only condition was that if I took the job I would meet the orchestra once a month because I do not believe in Chief Conductors who see the orchestra three times a year. I wanted to give the Phil a sound-image which was instantly recognisable. When you listened you would say 'Yes, that is Liverpool playing.' When I came I made a point of promoting music which was Czech. The audience liked it and asked for more. It was this repertoire, much of it recorded on CD which brought about the Liverpool Phil

being the first non-Czech orchestra to open the Prague Spring Festival in 1993. I was so proud of them and the manner in which they performed Bohemian music, it seemed only right that they should play in Prague. Right from the beginning, I found the members of the orchestra hard working and modest. I don't think they earn a fortune but there is something which keeps them here and which kept me here for so many years. When I first came my English was certainly not as good as it is now but, I find someone talking with a Scouse accent difficult to understand.

The Adelphi Hotel is my 'home' when I am in Liverpool. Despite all the criticism it has received, I still think it a most beautiful

119

place. I have more rapport with the maids and the porters than anyone else, though you don't see many porters today. The place used to be swarming with them. If the towels are slightly worn, there are other compensations. The maids are so nice and diligent, though goodness knows what they earn. Peanuts, I expect. When I am in Liverpool I follow more or less the same routine each day. I work at the Adelphi in the morning, then take a taxi from the front of the hotel to the concert hall. If I have an evening free, because there is no concert, I like to eat at an Indian restaurant – or I might take some fruit or 'junk' food back to my room.

There have been some very grand occasions at the Phil. In my time, the Queen came twice and the programme was suited to her taste– no long symphonies! I also met her in Prague when she knighted me in 1996. When we played in Seville Cathedral, Prince Charles was there with Diana. He spent some time sketching the interior of the Cathedral, during the concert.

Normally I fly into Manchester when I am coming to Liverpool but there have been times when I have driven overland from Prague, in my Land Rover. It takes two days because is it is more than one thousand miles. However I am travelling I come well equipped with clothes. If I am going to be here for fourteen days I bring sixteen pairs of socks and sixteen pairs of underpants, if there are five concerts, I bring six dress shirts, in case I perspire and need two shirts one night. The Adelphi will launder them the same day, if necessaary.

Unfortunately, much as I love Liverpool it has always meant work and schedules. There has never been time to look at it properly though obviously I have been to places like Penny Lane. After all I was very familiar with the Beatles music long before I came here. I love the Liverpool pubs: there is nothing like them – except for those in Dublin.

These days I have a gentleman's agreement with the Phil to be here for four weeks a year. The number of concerts is not specified – the important thing is that I see the orchestra regularly. That is a tremendous pleasure. When I am addressing them I call them 'Colleagues' because that is how I think of them. They call me 'Colleague' back – but it's a bit of a nickname.

No matter how often I come here, I never get tired of the city. Its funny really because when I have to leave Prague to travel to other places for my work I am reluctant to go. But when I am coming to Liverpool I cannot wait to get here.

One of these days, maybe when I retire I will come back for a holiday and really take a good look at all the places I have never had time to visit.

Libor Pesek (b. 1933) was Chief Conductor of the Royal Liverpool Philharmonic Orchestra from 1987 to 1997. He is now Conductor Laureate with the orchestra and lives in Prague.

Andrew and Liz Collinge on their way to fame and fortune.

What shall I be when I grow up? Andrew Collinge muses at five years of age.

We lived in West Derby when I was a small child and one of my first memories is of being in the hairdressing salon which my father, Peter Collinge, had in Hepworth Chambers, in Church Street, above where W.H. Smith's is now. I must have been about five or six and I was looking out of the window at the salon and watching the people go by. I can also remember the terrible fire at Henderson's, the department store opposite, in 1960, seeing the fire engines.

Another youthful memory is that my father made a stick with a magnet on the end and when I went to the salon with my mother, I used to pick up all the hairpins which had fallen on the floor. My parents ran the hairdressing business together. It was a natural progression. My grandfather had been a barber, my father went into ladies' hairdressing and by the early 1960s had become the Vidal Sassoon of the north. He was very much a pioneer, introducing cut and blow salons to the city. Of course hairdressing was a different thing in those days.My Dad tells a tale of how on the day he married my Mum he worked in the salon all morning before rushing off to church. These days some of the staff want a few days off before their wedding – not just a few hours!

At the Hepworth Chambers salon, John Anderson, my grandfather, my mother's father, looked after the office. Mum was on reception. It was a family business – still is. My sister Sarah, is a director.

My grandparents lived in Saxonia Road, Walton near Goodison Park and, when I was nine my grandfather took me to my first-ever football match to see Russia play Brazil in the 1966 World Cup. The great Pele was playing and was injured. The atmosphere was electric, amazing. We left West Derby when I was about five and went to live on the Wirral but as the hairdressing business operated from Liverpool we were in and out of the city all the time either travelling in my mother's bubble car through the Mersey Tunnel or on the ferry. In those days, the Mersey Tunnel had traffic lights and you could change lanes.

Then, I had no thoughts of going into hairdressing, but when I was eighteen I started brushing floors and shampooing clients at our West Kirby salon, as a holiday job, and became interested. As a result I joined one of the Liverpool salons. In 1976, I entered the Guild of Hairdressers Junior Competition at the Grafton Ballroom and got to the finals in London. Michael Rosser of Michael John, was one of the judges, and as I wanted to do the London thing, my Mum asked him if he would take me on. I came back to Liverpool in 1981 by which time I had married my wife, Liz.

One of the first people I shampooed at Michael John was Mrs Thatcher which I continued to do for two years. I clearly remember her asking me one day if I had voted in a local election. I said I could not be bothered. She turned round in mid-shampoo, absolutely soaking and told me people had fought and died to make Britain a democracy. She said she did not care how I voted but I must vote. It was such an intimidating experience that I have voted ever since.

At Michael John a lot of the clients were famous people including Princess Anne. Though I am very proud of my northern roots and the fact that our business is in the north-west, I do feel that a spell in London can have a major effect on your career and life. While I was there I began visiting Gatcombe Park to cut Princess Anne's children's hair, Zara and Peter Phillips. Since 1994 I have looked after the Countess of Wessex's hair.

In 1973 which was long before we knew much about Mrs Thatcher, my parents, of the opinion there was a need for younger, trendier hairdressing, in Liverpool, opened a new salon in Lime Street. They called it 'Thatchers' thinking of the hairdressing connection.

Andrew and Liz Collinge today.

It was near the old Virgin Records, which was the first regional Virgin shop in the country. 'Thatchers' was a fantastic success, with young people queuing round the block on Saturday, in the hope of a cancellation for a cut and blow dry. By the early 1980s, however, 'Thatcher' was not the most popular name, particularly in Liverpool and ultimately business did suffer in that particular salon. At the time there was a very depressed atmosphere within the city. You could not see how things were going to get better but fortunately they have and once again, it is a vibrant place to work and live.

Then, though Militant were in power, rates were sky high. There was an apprehension within the business community as to what the City Council were prepared to do. They seemed to want to take on the government at our expense. But there was regeneration for the city after the Toxteth Riots: notably the Albert Dock which ultimately became the home of the Maritime Museum, the Tate Gallery and the regional centre for Granada television news.

The national television programme, *This Morning*, hosted in Liverpool by Judy Finnegan and Richard Madely sprang into being in a studio opposite Fred's famous weather map. My wife Liz, and I were there from Day One doing make-overs on members of the public who wrote in looking for a change of image. We did over five hundred during the eight and a half years that the show went out from Liverpool.

Doing make-overs on *This Morning* was fun. Apart from what Liz and I did, it gave us the opportunity of meeting some very famous people. I don't honestly think Barry Manilow or other huge American stars understood that when they agreed to do a national daytime TV show, they would be leaving their hotel in London at the crack of dawn, coming up to Liverpool to have a chat, to go back again. But they did it, and they came back time and time again because they loved the show so much and they loved visiting the city. It was a shame when it moved to London.

For the last five years Liz, and I, have had a make-over salon at Harrods where we work one day every week but, our business remains a Liverpool one with headquarters and training academy in two Georgian houses we bought in Seymour Terrace, in the city centre. We've no thought of leaving. As a city Liverpool may be bit rough and ready but that is part of its charm.

Liverpoool definitely has a soul!

Andrew Collinge (b. 1956) runs the ten salons in the Andrew Collinge hairdressing organisation within the north as well as a training academy in Liverpool. He and his family live in Wirral.

CHAPTER 28
Debi Jones

Debi Jones today.

Debi in 1985.

Outsiders always seem intrigued as to what makes Liverpool tick. I think it may be because we are not afraid of making a fool of ourselves. We will tell anyone our life story. It angers me that Liverpool is thought of as a place full of downtrodden people living in a grotty area. I do not think we have had any more adversity than anywhere else though, of course, life today is very different from when I was a child.

The annual visit to the Christmas grottoes to tell Father Christmas what you wanted in your stocking was one of the highlights of the year for children like me, in the 1960s. My mother took my brother Roger, and myself to T.J. Hughes or Blacklers and I was always terrified of losing her because the city seemed so big. But she could zip

round Liverpool like nobody's business, so we held tight hold of her and followed close behind. Looking back the city seemed so much safer for children then, though that goes for most places.

By the time I was in my late teens and early twenties being in a group was all the rage. I was in one called Foxy Lady and wore Gary Glitter style boots and a silver mini skirt. We played rock music, Jimi Hendrix stuff. The theatre was popular: the Waterloo and Crosby Operatic Society could fill the Royal Court Theatre every night for a week. It was a tremendous thrill for me to play the lead in *The Merry Widow*, when I was eighteen. Because the theatre played such a dominant part in the city, the old theatrical digs were still around. I remember one run by a man called Walter

Scott in Bootle. He lived opposite, Jimmy Casey, son of Jimmy James, the comedian and later head of light entertainment, for BBC Radio. He had a wife I called Auntie Joan – Auntie Joan bought me a pair of red leather tap shoes, for my eighth birthday because she knew I wanted to be in show business.

By the time I went to Liverpool Institute of Higher Education to take a Bachelor of Education degree in 1981, Lark Lane was coming into its own as a fashionable, out of town place in which to eat. Keith's Wine Bar, which is still there, was a Mecca for students. For ninety pence you could get a fabulous salad, which was not just lettuce but had all sorts of interesting things in it. It was served with half a wholemeal loaf and a hunk of butter and kept you going all day. Then came L'Alouette – that was the posh place, with French food. You only went there about once a year unless you had a rich boyfriend. Young people took all sorts of jobs. When I was twenty-one, I worked in the advertising department at the Liverpool Echo. It was like being a battery hen and I hated it, so I did not stay. After I completed my degree, I went straight into radio, presenting the afternoon show on Radio Merseyside, which I loved.

Looking back Liverpool always had so many social clubs: The She, Wooky Hollow, Allinsons where I sometimes sang. People went to clubs like The She to have a drink and find someone to grapple with - cop off, as we say. So if you were belting out a Tina Turner song, it was purely background noise. It used to break my mother's heart because I was a trained opera singer. Blundells, the restaurant at the Bluecoat Chambers was more upmarket and attracted a lovely clientele. I earned £10 a night singing there when I was a student – or could have a fiver and a meal for two. I was in great demand.

All my memories of Liverpool are career orientated. On Radio Merseyside I did the two-till-five show for five years. There was a show called 'School's Out' and you'd ask youngsters to ring in and tell you where the quote 'Out damned spot' came from. They'd come back with answers like 'The Woodentots' or 'Adrian Mole.'.

These days I owe most of my allegiance to a different area in Liverpool – the Albert Dock and Granada Television where you will find Britain's first home grown shopping channel called Shop! It is run by Littlewoods and Granada. We, who work there, love the Albert Dock. The whole area has been a tremendous asset to Liverpool. Visitors are amazed at the beauty of the Granada Studio, which is a listed building. So is the Pump House next door which was restored to its original state and is now the pub used by the media. Frank and Jill, the landlords are always happy to let Granada have 'props' – a bucket of ice or bottle of port – if they need them for a particular television show. It's the equivalent of the old idea of borrowing a cup of sugar.

Liverpool's future seems to look bright, but we do have to stop living in the past. Take Hillsborough, for instance: it was probably the worst thing that ever happened to Liverpool but we have to move on. People from other cities are sick of hearing about it. It was dreadful, it was unforgivable, but we have to put it behind

Debi in 1990.

I firmly believe that here in Liverpool, as anywhere else, you can make something of your life, if you wish. That said, I would never live anywhere else. When I go to London I feel like a very small fish in the Atlantic Ocean. I am always glad to get back to Lime Street. In the future I'd like to buy a bolt hole in Spain or France but Liverpool will always be home.

I would never leave it.

Debi Jones (b. 1959) is the presenter of SHOP!, Littlewoods' and Granada Television's shopping channel. She lives in Crosby.

us, and hopefully when all the court cases are over, we'll be able to.

There are a great many hard working folk in the city but all we hear about are those who buck the system. There is a strata here who think the world owes them a living, but they are by no means in the majority and they occur in every major city.

Of course, it would be grand for everyone to have a job for life, but we have to get real. We have to look at things differently. That might have been the case when there was no automation, when there were pit ponies and we were dependent on physical labour and manpower. But that world was not particularly beautiful either.